CHALMERS ROBERTS still contributes to the *Washington Post*, where he was an award-winning reporter, then chief diplomatic correspondent until 1971. The author of three previous books, he lives with his wife in Bethesda, Maryland.

Chalmers M. Roberts

HOW DID I GET HERE SO FAST?

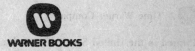

WARNER BOOKS

A Time Warner Company

WARNER BOOKS EDITION

Cover design by Janet Perr

Warner Books, Inc.
1271 Avenue of the Americas
New York, N.Y. 10020

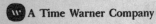 A Time Warner Company

Printed in the United States of America

Originally published in hardcover by Warner Books.
First printed in paperback: August, 1992

10 9 8 7 6 5 4 3 2 1

For
Lois
and
for
David and Mary
Patricia and David
Christopher and Mary
(confusing, isn't it?)
and
for
Rebecca
Matthew
Kevin
Morgan
Kathryn
Rachel
and
Sarah

Contents

Preface . . . . *xi*
Matthew *1*
Baby Boomers *5*
What a Way to Retire! *15*
Christopher *27*
The Big Seven-Oh *33*
How Old Is Old? *45*
On Hitting Eighty *61*
Picket-Guard at Ninety *79*
Mystic Chords of Memory *95*
Plato vs. Eros *115*
Chance or Plan? *125*
Sources *139*
Acknowledgments *159*

I CONCEIVED THIS BABY years ago, and fortunately my wife was of an age that we didn't have to go to the hospital, so we had it right in the publisher's office.

It feels like flesh and love, and there're plenty of both here. But truly, it's about our later years, about growing older, and how to sandwich in some real life between medical appointments. Yes, it's a feel-good, or at least a feel-better, book, and along the route there's some looking back, in a friend's phrase, with grace and energy.

Time is our most important asset. So let's get on with our story.

C.M.R.
Age 80
(How did I get here so fast?)

Preface

THE YEAR BEFORE HE RE-
tired at 91 as the oldest justice ever to sit on
the Supreme Court of the United States,
Oliver Wendell Holmes, Jr., and his close
friend Justice Louis Brandeis, then a mere
74, were out for one of their frequent con-
stitutionals on Washington's Capitol Hill.

The year was 1931, back in the era
before the Court abandoned its small and
intimate quarters on the ground floor of the
Capitol Building for the vast marble palace
across the street. For Holmes and Brandeis a
daily walk was part of their established order, a time to shrug off judicial problems, to

get a bit of fresh air, sunshine, and exercise, to share tales, to reminisce.

On this particular day, so goes this oft-told tale, the justices spotted a pretty girl approaching them, perhaps with "a well-turned ankle" in a phrase of their youth. Or, as a modern account has it, they saw "an attractive young blonde mince across their path."

Holmes "paused, sighed," and said to Brandeis:

"Oh, to be seventy again!"

On his own seventieth birthday Holmes had written to a friend, asking him to "give my love" to his wife. "Tell her the old man swept round the last post to the home stretch going strong."

Wendell Holmes, as he was called, lived to within two days of his ninety-fourth birthday. And on that birthday President Franklin D. Roosevelt stood bareheaded in sleet and cold at graveside in Arlington National Cemetery.

This is not, however, a book about Holmes, although there will be more about him. Rather, it is a book about approaching 70, the day you become 70, and about the years that follow. It is a book, especially, for those still hard at work—including the baby boomers—for those who avoid the very idea of "aging," indeed detest that word, yet who are beginning to pause long enough to contemplate retirement, even to prepare for what Walt Whitman described as "the grandeur and exquisiteness of old age." Of course, Whitman was only 41 when he wrote that.

Matthew

MY WIFE'S LEFT ELBOW caught me in the right rib cage. A second poke and I got the point. There is no mistaking the cry of a hungry baby in the middle of the night. My feet slowly edged out from under the covers into slippers, my arms rose into my robe. As I struggled to stand up, I could see Matthew through the doorway, standing in his neck-to-toes pajamas, his blond head peering over the near end of the crib he was grasping with both hands, his mouth contorted in a wail of total unhappiness at this god-awful moment in the tenth month of his life.

Now, this scene has been repeated ad

1

infinitum since Adam and Eve had Cain and Abel, or at least since beds, cribs, and Dr. Denton's were invented, most especially since rubber-nippled milk bottles for kids began. The difference at this particular moment in human history was that I was not Matthew's father but his grandfather; he was my eldest son's son. It was 1984, and I was 73, and at this time of night every bone in my body seemed to creak as I hung on to the railing, creeping down the steep staircase to fetch the kid's bottle from the fridge, then to begin climbing Everest once again.

His parents were in Florida, attending— believe me—the Eleventh World Orchid Conference. His sister, Rebecca, six, was tucked in her own dreamworld in the room next door. And my wife, Lois, had gone back to sleep, if she had ever really awakened.

So there I was sitting in an old-fashioned high-back rocking chair, clad only in my floor-length, Sherlock Holmes, red-lined, plaid bathrobe, wearing a Santa Claus red hat with a white-ball tassel. Matthew's head lay cradled in the crook of my right arm—I'm a southpaw—his bottle balanced by my left hand as he slurped away. Outside his bedroom windows an early-March snowfall diffused the silent streetlight's glow.

HOW DID I GET HERE SO FAST?

Since only Matthew could hear me, I was free to indulge in my totally monotone variations of nursery rhymes as I gently rocked away.

Matthew was obligingly oblivious. My mind wandered. My eyes canvassed his room, focused on nothing. Then the thought struck me: what in the hell is a 73-year-old man doing at five o'clock in the morning rocking a baby, his mouth plugged with a milk bottle's nipple, in the middle of a snowstorm with nobody else giving a damn?

When is it that your mind wanders? Listening to a symphony? Swimming laps in a pool? Floating in a canoe? Or feeding a baby? Whatever, the results can be some of your best thoughts and ideas. I began to consider grandfather and grandson.

In Matthew's case, you might say that he and I represented an act of love, a reciprocated grandfatherly love. Indeed, Lois and I found ourselves doing something akin for our other grandchildren, including the surprise twins and Rebecca. It simply runs with human nature. Lois enjoyed broadening Rebecca's finicky tastes by introducing her to swordfish. But I made a tactical error, after she had fallen for french fries, by mentioning that they were made of potatoes. Ergo, no more fries.

Bonding is today's word. That love was there that night between me and Matthew, in the warmth we brought each other, I'm sure. But a lot more, too. We grandparents wish we might be around to see each baby develop, to know how he or she turns out a decade or two hence when his or her own persona has been fully formed. Since that can be chancy, we fall back on our own imaginations, compare baby pictures, extrapolate from the child's form, gestures, sounds, indeed his or her style. "As the twig is bent, so the tree's inclined," it used to say in the stained-glass window of my high school stairwell. Look for signs of inclinations; they're usually there.

Matthew, for instance, has been fascinating to watch. Here's a way station when he reached 4 and I was 77.

MATTHEW: "Grandfather, you look awfully old."

GRANDFATHER: "How old do you think I am?"

MATTHEW (after reflection): "Nineteen."

Baby Boomers

SOMETHING CLOSE TO a third of all Americans are baby boomers. By a recent reckoning that's nearly 80 million out of over 250 million of all ages. What is a baby boomer? The generally accepted definition is someone born in America between January 1, 1947, and December 31, 1964, although the Census Bureau, which likes to count its years from July through June 30, favors starting on July 1, 1946.

At any rate, these are the children conceived in the wake of World War II, when millions of servicemen, and a goodly number of servicewomen, were separated from their spouses. In case you've forgotten, the war in Europe against Hitler's Nazis ended on May 7, 1945, and the war in Asia against Japan ended, after the atomic bombs on Hiroshima and Nagasaki, on August 15. Add nine months, probably plus some more to allow for time to reach home, get married, if you weren't already, and start planning a family. The boom went on for an incredible eighteen years.

In a way, I feel like the Big Daddy of the baby boomers because Lois and I have three of them, now all in their forties. David, the eldest, the fellow who stands between Matthew and me, was born on February 4, 1947, which puts him pretty close to the beginning of this formidable human tide. Oddly, as we all discovered during the 1988 Republican convention, J. Danforth (Dan) Quayle was born the very same day of the very same year. Not being of the same political persuasion, my David, with some anguish, phoned me to ask what hour of that day he'd been born. It was 6:10 P.M. Eastern time in Washington, D.C. Nowadays when you ask Vice President Quayle's office for the hour of his birth, you're told: "We don't have the hour. We just have the day." Probably somebody's worrying about a potentially bad horoscope.

Anyway, the first of the baby boomers are now in their forties, millions more are reaching 40 each year, although the babiest baby boomer won't get there until 2004, using that generally accepted definition.

The oldest boomers are already feeling their age. How else do you account for the jubilation in print and on the air in 1990 when (1) Nolan Ryan, the 43-year-old Texas Ranger, pitched his sixth no-hitter; (2) George Foreman, the 41-year-old boxer, knocked out his opponent in the second round; and (3) Hale Erwin, the 45-year-old golfer, won his third U.S. Open championship. And then there is Dan Quayle, inaugurated vice president of the United States at 41. (Teddy Roosevelt became vice president at 42; John Breckinridge, the youngest, at a mere 36.)

I guess it's a fact, as my medical encyclopedia says, that "the shock of realization that one is no longer young" comes to "most Americans sometime between 40 and 50." This is the time of life, baby boomers, when a lot of you will begin worrying about "changes in appearance, stamina, sexual function, emotions, memory, and intelligence." Skin, for example, "gradually becomes drier and thinner." As to sexual abstinence, it can lead to impotence; i.e., use it or lose it.

Ryan, Foreman, and Erwin all show what man can do if he tries hard enough and has some well-honed skills. But lots of baby boomers are not in that kind of shape; in fact, 40 or so is a "great" year to be an overweight, high-blood-pressure, couch-potato candidate for a midlife heart attack. Even quite a few athletes manage to drop dead from too strenuous exercise, although it's often because they had some hitherto undetected malady.

My point here is simply that baby boomers better look out, and for at least two reasons:

One, they themselves are beginning to look at that big sign down the road proclaiming "50" or "Half a Century," and a lot of them have started to wonder how they got so close so fast. They may even be thinking about retirement, certainly about their prospective retirement benefits.

Two, they will be finding themselves part of what has been called "the sandwich generation," that is, those who are caught between still raising children at home or getting them through college while beginning to have to look after aging, sometimes suddenly ill, parents.

HOW DID I GET HERE SO FAST?

Some of the old who live in arctic cultures, we're told, simply walk out into the gloom of ice and fog to die, having served their human purpose and not wanting, or not being allowed, to be a burden their society cannot bear. A governor of Colorado a while back suggested that maybe some old Americans, too, might take a walk of sorts, shuffle out of the way of the baby boomers, quit eating up the latter's legacies with medical bills and their substance in paying those social security taxes for the oldsters' support. In Britain, it's customary not to accept people over 55 who develop kidney disease as dialysis patients. In Sweden, some hospitals won't recommend surgery for cancer patients over 75, heart patients over 70. And here in America, there's lots of talk of somehow "rationing" expensive health care for the aged.

The 1990 Supreme Court decision on the "right to die" issue puts it up to oldsters to provide "clear and convincing" proof in advance if they don't want their bodies to be sustained beyond their sentient lives by the tubes, machines, and chemicals of modern medicine. "Living wills" are the new in-thing for senior citizens.

Maybe it's worth mentioning here a

word or two about those "greedy geezers" we often read about, the old folks, retired, who haven't shuffled off. They're pictured as living it up on social security paid for by those ever-rising taxes on the baby boomers and now also by the younger generations following along behind the boomers.

One day I was at the dentist—he then was 41—and we got talking (he did the talking; I did the mumbling) about then-president Reagan's cuts in social spending and attacks on social security. It turned out my dentist had never even heard of a county poorhouse. For him and for the bulk of other Americans the social safety net seemed always to have been in place. 'Tweren't so.

I remember a maudlin song titled "Over the Hill to the Poorhouse." And I remember Dad taking me in the 1920s to visit the Cambria County, Pennsylvania, poor farm where the otherwise homeless and infirm, as well as the retarded, helped support themselves by tilling the fields and picking the crops. I particularly remember a room, straw on the floor, full of incontinent children, the products of coal miner incest. And in the county seat, Ebensburg, as in many an American town, the older kids teased and sometimes physically abused the so-called town idiot. Today we would recognize him or her as a retarded person.

Out of the Great Depression of the 1930s and Franklin D. Roosevelt's New Deal came the Social Security Act of 1936. My records show that twenty-five cents was deducted from my first 1937 pay envelope when I was working in Toledo, Ohio. And yes, I'm still paying social security taxes on what profit I make from writing articles or books such as this one, though for the past eighteen years I've been receiving retirement benefits in far, far larger amounts than what I paid in. These benefits are the so-called entitlements, and my wife (who also paid those taxes and now also draws these benefits) and I have been paying income taxes in recent years on half of our total social security take.

Now I know it seems, and is, outrageous for the very rich to be getting social security, but most of the tales about such cases are in the same category as Ronald Reagan's stories about the "welfare queen" driving in a Cadillac to pick up her welfare checks. They are true anecdotally but are not significant statistically; most everyone on social security needs that money to live on decently. We do.

Most of us oldsters consider our social security payments a pension, though they are, arguably, welfare payments: a transfer of funds from working Americans to retired Americans. Or from our children with jobs to their parents who've quit working.

But the terminology is less important than the facts. Charles Krauthammer, a conservative columnist of great skill, has made this point:

> When Bismarck created the West's first old-age pension in Germany a century ago, he picked 65 as the retirement age. The choice was as cunning as it was arbitrary: hardly anyone made it to 65 then. When FDR created Social Security 50 years later, median U.S. life expectancy was 63.7 years. The average retiree was already dead.
>
> Of course, the relevant number is not life expectancy at birth but at retirement age. In the late 1930s those already 65 could expect to live another 12½ years. In 2020, life expectancy at 65 will be 19 years.

Which, of course, is why Republican Reagan and the Democratically controlled Congress had to agree to raise social security taxes to cover the big benefits that will be paid down the road to the baby boomers. And it's why the social security "fund" nowadays is so massive, building up as it awaits those boomer retirements and the long retirement years during which they will be entitled to draw monthly checks. By 2030 the entire baby boom generation will be 65 or older, most of them drawing social security even if the first check, by then, has been delayed until you're, say, 67.

My children, probably like yours if you're retired, have been longtime skeptics about ever receiving social security, and some of them also bellyache about the big bite it takes out of their earnings. The tax is regressive; income ought to be fully taxable; probably other changes in the law should be made. But the reason for social security is as sound today as when FDR proposed it, and the necessity for it is growing even greater because of our aging population. When all the baby boomers have reached 65, they and their living predecessors will account for nearly 21 percent of our total population, or so the estimates now show. And that's more than double the percentage of the 1960 census.

Remember, when Shakespeare wrote "The Seven Ages of Man" he was only 35 or 36. But what perceptions!

All the world's a stage
And all the men and women merely players.
They have their exits and their entrances,
And one man in his time plays many parts . . .

THE LINOTYPE

What a Way to Retire!

For MOST OF US RETIRE-tirement is a personal, largely private thing. Mine, at age 60, had been planned just that way, but took a sudden, very different turn. On the very day I had long set to be my last one at work, I was freed of the threat of going to jail for having participated in something the federal government contended could cause "injury of the United States to the advantage of a foreign nation." And I was freed that day by none other than the Supreme Court of the United States.

What a way to retire! No doubt, I was luckier than most because my retirement scenario reassured me I would still be able to keep on writing for pay, though at a lesser price. Slow leave-taking from the work world is not all that unusual nowadays when you think of how many Americans are disengaging from their careers. The average age of retirement is getting younger every year; it's now down to 62. Lots of people arrange partial retirement or limited hours per day or flextime or work at home via computer. Gradual release of the ties that bind you to the desk, the counter, or the assembly line certainly makes the transition easier to take. Retirement from a full-time job produces a certain strain; and after you've organized all the incredible paperwork that goes with it, you'll probably find a gap in your days that steady work has filled for so many years.

The key to retirement is how you do it. Some can quit cold turkey. I had a friend who swore he was going fishing; he actually did. Another walked out of the office to say he'd never set foot again in that damned place; he was murdered two weeks later by an intruder in his new Florida apartment. And I had a friend who worked on happily for years until he finally died at an even 100.

For most of us, retirement is a turning point of life, a point at which focus and lifestyle change, sometimes drastically, especially in the matter of income. Forced early retirements greatly increased in the era of leveraged buyouts and of companies, for whatever reasons, determined to be "lean and mean." "Lean" can mean a very personal trauma. But some people simply don't retire. Lawyers hate to give up their offices (one we know still uses his, and his part-time secretary, to pursue his Civil War hobby), and federal judges get to go on something called senior status (at full pay provided they go on working) where, if they're clever, they can be assigned to Puerto Rico or San Diego to hear cases in January and February.

As for me, I was all ready for retirement from daily journalism after thirty-eight years in the newspaper business. Everybody at my paper, the *Washington Post*, knew I was about to leave. I'd even received my farewell gift—my office chair with a bronze plaque affixed to its back full of kind words of praise. Then, bango! On June 17, 1971, only thirteen days from my official retirement date, it fell to me to write a story that represented the gut issue of my entire professional career—freedom of the press.

The New York Times had hit the doorsteps on June 13 with masses of text from and about the hitherto secret Pentagon Papers, the government's own account of how and why the U.S. had gotten into the war in Vietnam, and the subsequent twists, turns, deceptions, and lies as they developed through the end of the Lyndon Johnson administration.

Four days after the *Times* broke the Pentagon Papers story, my paper obtained most of the same documents. The *Times* by then had been ordered by a federal court to halt publication of its material, and this "prior restraint" had resulted in a struggle in the courts between the press and the government, with interpretation of the first amendment ("Congress shall make no law . . . abridging the freedom . . . of the press") its core issue. At the home of *Post* executive editor Benjamin C. Bradlee on the afternoon and evening of June 17, two other reporters and I wrote stories in a feverish effort to catch up with our New York rival. We'd been warned not to publish; the question was: should we? If we decided to go ahead, the first story we published would be mine.

While we reporters were busy writing, the *Post*'s lawyers were in the next room talking about holding off and giving Attorney General John Mitchell a warning that we, too, had the Pentagon Papers and planned to print something a day or two later. All the reporters, and those of our editors who were present, exploded. In fact, I remember declaring hotly that such a move amounted to "crawling on your belly to the attorney general." If the *Post* did so, I added, with difficulty in restraining my emotions, I would issue a public statement disassociating myself from the action. And I would move up my retirement and stop working then and there.

Now, today, this may all sound like something out of *The Front Page* or some other journalistic melodrama. But we were deadly serious. I guess I felt as though the Bill of Rights, under which I had worked so long, was at stake. Remember, they used to say of newspapermen, they don't get paid much except in bylines, known as the psychic wage. And those bylines represented your reputation. I was defending mine.

Of course, the *Post* went on to publish my story that night, and after we had run a second story the next day, the paper was enjoined by the courts from further publication. The *Times,* the *Post,* and some others all wound up before the "Supremes," the handy short term for the nine justices of the Supreme Court of the United States. They handed down their decision, overruling the government on prior restraint, on what turned out to be my preplanned last day of office work, June 30, 1971.

Well, it was some way to resign. I have framed on my office wall at home a "mat" of the next day's front page with the eight-column headline "Court Rules for Newspapers, 6–3," and three more stories extracted from those Pentagon Papers. (Perhaps I should explain that the framed "mat" is a sort of cardboard or papier-mâché mold made by being pressed against the metal type. The mat is used to make a curved, lead stereotype plate that is put on the presses to print the page onto newsprint. It's all now a long-gone, obsolete technology in this age of computers.) On the back of my frame, along with the old clippings, is a copy of the government's chilling document, formally entitled *United States of America, plaintiff* v. *The Washington Post Company,* and then the names of all thirteen of its top officials plus my name bringing up the rear as the fourteenth "defendant."

I don't think it ever really occurred to me that if we had lost the case before the Supreme Court, we all might have ended up in jail. The jail part was probably unlikely, although not impossible. But the government pressure on the press felt like one of those 600-pound gorillas sitting on your chest.

Well, as you can imagine, it took me some time to come off that emotional high. For some days I kept on going into the office to clean out my desk and filing cabinets, to bring much home, toss much into the trash baskets. It didn't take long for me to realize that life—the business of putting out a daily newspaper—was going on all around me. And that my absence didn't make a damned bit of difference.

I was luckier than most after retiring, for the paper kept printing my pieces— thirteen over the rest of that year, forty-nine the next year, and so on in diminishing numbers as I managed to get weaned. But not totally. In 1990—remember I retired in mid-1971—I had two pieces published. Many of these articles were based on ideas I suggested to the editor; others, including book reviews, they suggested to me. And as time went along, I found that some of the things I wrote were being spiked, that is, not used. More of the weaning process.

Of course, I wrote other things, too:

magazine pieces, a couple of books. One book was pretty much an autobiography, the other the centennial history of my newspaper. Writing a book, such as the one you're reading now, calls for a very different frame of mind from writing for a daily paper. I used to do the Washington column for the *Atlantic Monthly,* and it was a very good exercise for me because I had to stand back and look at a subject with perspective, at least with a great deal more perspective than when writing for a seven P.M. deadline. Writing a book requires an even longer perspective. Hey, writing one like this draws on your whole life's perspective.

I'm not sure how conscious I was at the time of this "perspective" process. Many years later I discovered the right way to describe it. John Bartlow Martin, long a heavy hitter for the *Saturday Evening Post* in its glory years, put it this way in his autobiography: let the story "marinate" in your mind because writers usually begin to write "too soon, before we have really digested the material." *Marinate* is exactly the right word.

Sometimes in retirement there is too much time for marination, and sitting around thinking can become just sitting around. For most wives, those who have retired from work outside the home or those who simply worked at home, there is still a lot to do in the daily routine of running a household. The sitting-around husband may become "a man under-foot." That's no kidding; I've heard wives complain about situations like this.

In my case, my wife, Lois, having sold her bookshop at the time I retired, used her head and energies on other pursuits: the garden, painting, and for some years volunteer tutoring of kids with learning problems. Lois also did a wonderful thing for me: she turned what had been the kids' small ground-floor playroom into my office. She bought me bookcases and stained them, repaired the asphalt-tile flooring, and repainted the battered green walls a bright yellow. It took exactly three coats of yellow to obliterate the green, she remembers to this day. The lock on the door to this room remains busted, for sentimental reasons. I haven't had it fixed because I like to think of it as a memento of the kids' occupancy. You see, the older boy busted it one day when his younger brother teasingly locked it from the inside. Boys do that sort of thing; our daughter was always too much a lady for such carryings-on, but she knew how to play one brother against the other.

In short, in retirement neither of us was around under the other's feet. We each had our own busy ways. That's an ideal you should try for. Of course, as your vim and vigor slow, those extra activities tend to be curbed or even ended. Pace yourself; slow down gradually.

There's another thing I've found more interesting than I thought it might be. I've tried unsuccessfully to get my wife, who herself has written some delightful pieces for the *Washington Post,* to do one on how to introduce your husband to the kitchen, now that he's retired. There are a lot of retired husbands I've known who never took to the kitchen. Oh, yes, now they would fix the drinks or pass the cheese-and-crackers tray, but the little lady kept on doing her thing in the kitchen. Dinner appeared, eureka! Unfair, and unsettling to retirement marriages, in my book.

It may be true that you, man, couldn't boil water when you retired. Now you can at least make dinner salads, the luncheon sandwiches, the juice-and-toast breakfast. It's no great pain. And if you do much of the shopping, it gives you the chance for that great male thing—impulse buying, and you can bring home some extra goodies that your wife would never have dreamed of buying. Gradually, you work yourself into the kitchen. In time, I'm even learning to cook this or that (I already have a passing grade on most vegetables), and I don't mean just opening frozen-dinner boxes and plunging the plastic bags into boiling water.

After all, since we have both life and liberty, the retirement biggie is happiness. But not just Emerson's definition: "To fill the hour—that is happiness." Too limited. As I look at it, the Founding Fathers had it just right when they described it as "the pursuit of happiness." Never quit pursuing.

Christopher

BACK IN JULY 1961 THE nation's Civil War buffs began four years of centennial observations by recreating the First Battle of Manassas, as the South called it, the First Bull Run as the North knew it. The anniversary day turned out to be incredibly steamy, probably worse than the original as far as the temperature went, but the men in blue and gray sweated through their reenactment of the Yankee disaster with soldierly grit.

I drove my three—David, then 14, Patricia, 13, and Christopher, 10—as did thousands of other parents, across the Potomac to the Virginia battle site, now a fascinating national park. If we couldn't see history in its original, as the Northern sightseers a century early had sought to do by jauntily riding out from Washington in their carriages or on horseback, then at least let's not miss the second time round, now an easy car drive.

We even joined in a sort of replay of those 1861 tourists who had to scurry back to the capital lest they be enveloped in the fighting. We had to retreat, too, not in rout but in sweat. The kids and I talked about the battle and the war as I tried to sketch for them the larger meaning. Chris, already a history buff, had evidently been playing around in his mind with the concept of a century; remember, he was ten.

When we reached home, my wife, Lois, asked how it had been, and we all gave our centennial accounts. Chris stopped for a moment, then asked his mother how old *she* was. When she was honest enough to tell him, his wide-eyed reply was: "Mommy, you're half as old as the Civil War."

Nearly thirty years later, when Christopher's oldest son, Kevin, was just short of six, he acquired the concept of one hundred. He gave me this explanation: "I love Morgan [his younger brother] one hundred, I love Rachel and Sarah [his new twin sisters] one hundred"—and with a smile—"and I love you one hundred." The percent stuff, like the concept of a century, would come later on. Right then I got one hundred in its purest form.

As a high schooler studying Latin, I could read in the original Cicero's famous essay on old age, *De Senectute*. Now I have to read it in English, showing that the slippage of age is not just my usual short-term-memory problem.

In his reasons "why old age is regarded as unhappy," Marcus Tullius Cicero (106–43 B.C.), who wrote this at 62, cited as number one: "Old age withdraws us from active employments." How true today for so many. But does it have to be so? No, reasoned Cicero. "Large affairs are not performed by muscle, speed, nimbleness, but by reflection, character, judgment. In age, these qualities are not diminished but augmented."

How's that for making you feel good?

Remember Justice Holmes. And consider Winston Churchill, Charles de Gaulle, Konrad Adenauer, Deng Xiaoping, Ronald Reagan. All led major nations well into their old age. But in each of these cases it is also true that their latter years in power certainly were not their best. Only Deng is still at it, and a banner carried in Tiananmen Square before the 1989 crackdown read: "Deng Xiaoping, when people are past 80 years old, they get muddleheaded."

Cicero's reason number two for old age being "unhappy" was the fact that age "impairs physical vigor." Some of those just named attest to one reason, some to the other, some to both cited by Cicero. Cicero himself was murdered at 63; many of his fellow upper-class Romans are now believed to have died young because they ate from fancy plates made of lead, suffering slow but deadly lead poisoning.

Old age as a concept linked to particular years keeps shifting, always has apparently. Perhaps our standard was set way back around 150 B.C. in the Old Testament words of Psalms 90:10: "The days of our years are threescore and ten"—70. But don't forget that the psalm goes on to say: "and if by reason of strength they be fourscore years, yet is their strength labor and sorrow; for it is soon cut off, and we fly away."

Not so fast! Let us linger at 70, at least keep our minds there. Anything, almost, is possible. Consider these lovely anonymous lines:

HOW DID I GET HERE SO FAST?

King Solomon and King David
Led very merry lives,
With very many concubines
And very many wives,
Until old age came creeping,
With very many qualms,
Then Solomon wrote the Proverbs,
And David wrote the Psalms.

The Big
Seven-Oh

Musicians, especially orchestra leaders, as a class seem to live longer than any other group. Remember Toscanni, Koussevitzky, Stokowski, Ormandy, Fiedler—yes, Irving Berlin. The composer Aaron Copland, who died at 90, did a lot of orchestra conducting in his eighties, saying that it helped keep him young: "You have an athletic workout—you come off the stage sweating like a pig."

But I've never seen any statistics on the longevity of journalists. Nothing like musicians, for sure. Some years back it seemed that almost daily I was sitting at a memorial service for a colleague. At the last service in that series, the journalist next to me, who'd also been at the others, turned to me and said: "Chal, this has got to stop." I agreed. He was dead in two weeks.

Today Americans are living longer, on the average. Take presidents. Once many of us thought Dwight D. Eisenhower terribly old to be president; he was ninety-eight days past 70 when he *left* the White House after eight years. But the next eight-year occupant, Ronald W. Reagan, was seventeen days short of 70 when he *entered* the White House. Not one of the thirty-eight other men who have served as president reached 70 while in office. George Herbert Walker Bush, however, will be 72 if he completes two full terms.

So, let's say that you have now retired. And that you did it in your sixties. Probably they had a retirement party for you at the office, or whatever. I don't think many gold watches get handed out these days; more likely, a sheet of paper listing retirement benefits and how to apply for them, including that very valuable health insurance. Never overlook that health insurance.

And then you see 70 coming up, that biblical three score and ten. (Forget about Methuselah, a biblical patriarch said to have lived 969 years. That story made a stirring ballad, but 969 is not for us. Forget, too, those yogurt-eating over-100 folks in the rugged mountain areas of Iran, Soviet Georgia, and eastern Turkey. Come back to reality.) We're talking here of people just reaching 70, the chronological age, not the physical or mental age. When you made 70, you beat the odds that existed when you were born. Many of your contemporaries won't make it.

If your family, your kids, your friends, don't throw a bash for you at 70, order one up for yourself. I did. Imagine: printed invitations have been mailed; a big spread has been ordered at your home or at a restaurant; drinks, champagne probably, are on order; maybe fillets of beef, maybe mesquite-grilled chicken, maybe a feast of crabmeat, whatever's your favorite. Spare no expense. Dad is only 70 once.

Dad? Well, did you ever hear of throwing a seventieth bash for Mom? Yes, it does happen; my sister-in-law threw one for herself. But that's a rarity. Women seem to want to hide their age, men to flaunt it, at least by 70. An easy way out for both to celebrate is at a golden wedding anniversary, assuming you married young enough and didn't switch spouses along the way.

Some kids say "twenty stinks" or "turning thirty stinks." Remember "Don't trust anyone over thirty"? Today "thirty-something" is a mask for the toughest birthday, 40. Forty, I guess, is too traumatic for some, a midlife crisis for others. But you get over it, even get over those ribbing greeting cards that usually come with it. Who marks 50? Jack Nicklaus did. He was described as uptight until he won his first senior professional golf tournament. Then he relaxed, had the biggest payday of his career—$1 million—and started to joke about getting into movies cheaper and receiving senior citizen discounts at hotels. For many who don't have their eyes focused on the ball as well as does Nicklaus, however, 50 can lead to asking one's self: Half a century and what have I accomplished? Banish the thought. You can, however, play it safe and join the American Association of Retired People (one third of whose 32 million members are still working!) and start receiving some discounts on medicines and other things. At 55, a bank ad says, all its fiscal goodies are now "for you who lived through cod-liver oil, platform shoes, diaper pails, and 55 Miss America pageants." As to reaching 60, it's an age hard to hide. If you're not already talking retirement, somebody in your workplace may be talking it up for you when they scan the payroll.

HOW DID I GET HERE SO FAST?

But 70! Oh, to be 70 again!

The seventieth bash is great. People say nice things about you, lie about you a bit, maybe a lot, even outrageously. They make you feel good, sometimes even make you blubber. Sometimes, too, you'll be surprised at what your own kids will say out loud in front of everybody, pleasantly surprised to the point of making it seem that all those years nurturing them have been, after all, worth the trial and travail.

And you get to sum up life's laws learned, or whatever, provided you don't carry on to the point of boring all assembled, z-z-z-z. Remember Andy Warhol's rule: everybody's entitled to fifteen minutes in the spotlight, but no more.

If your grandchildren are big enough, they are surely filming all this, in color and with sound. This is today's equivalent of the tintypes of our grandparents. After the first showing, though, who will ever see those films again? Will they be squirreled away in some case the way the tintypes were tucked into old bread boxes?

Or maybe your grandchildren, when they grow up, will rediscover such stuff in that King Tut's tomb in the attic (if they still have attics then) and find the show intriguing, maybe even hilarious enough for one of those ancient family video shows on television. Hope so.

Of course, the seventies are not necessarily all smooth sailing. Take Benjamin Franklin, for instance, and his gout. He wrote this "Dialogue Between Franklin and the Gout" in French when he was 73:

> "Let us examine your course of life," the Gout said. "When the mornings are long and you have plenty of time to go out for a walk, what do you do? Instead of getting up an appetite for breakfast by salutary exercise, you amuse yourself with books, pamphlets, and newspapers, most of which are not worth the trouble. Yet you eat an abundant breakfast, not less that four cups of tea with cream, and one or two slices of buttered toast covered with strips of smoked beef . . . Immediately afterward you sit down to write at your desk or talk with people who come to you on business. This lasts until an hour after noon, without any kind of bodily exercise . . . But what do you do after

dinner? Instead of walking in the beautiful gardens of the friends with whom you have dined, like a man of sense, you settle down at the chessboard, and there you stay for two or three hours. . . ."

Franklin: "Ah! How tiresome you are. . . . Oh! Oh! For heaven's sake leave me! And I promise faithfully that from now on I shall play no more chess but shall take daily exercise and live temperately."

Gout: "I know you too well. You promise beautifully; but after a few months of good health, you will go back to your old habits; your fine promises will be forgotten like the forms of last year's clouds."

Now I've had gout myself. It's a form of arthritis that, for unknown reasons, attacks only males and it's very painful. Fortunately, there are medicines nowadays that quickly relieve the pain. Alas, however, gout, which usually hits you first in a quickly swelling big toe, is associated with red wine and red meat, which is why upper-class British males were, and still are, gout victims. They say that besides Franklin other notable sufferers have been Achilles, Ulysses, Henry VIII, Charles Darwin, Isaac Newton, and Alexander Hamilton.

We pay for our sins. When gout first hit me about the age it hit Franklin, I could only sigh and remember all that lovely bordeaux and burgundy I'd drunk over the years. But with a switch in medicines, I'm now able to hoist a glass of red again, thank God, though I'm cautious about it. Maybe less cautious, however, since I read about a French study showing that three or four glasses of red wine a day reduced the risk for men of having a heart attack.

We oldsters, also, on occasion, don't act our age. Lois and I visited Disney World in Florida when I was 71, and we were attracted by one of those rides through Wild West country. But at the last minute she chickened out. I wish I had, too. Instead, I played macho, found myself on a roller coaster with wild whirls and jerky turns, my heart thumping, afraid I'd be tossed out. Insane.

Or take Mt. Rubidoux in California, at the edge of Riverside, which is about fifty miles east of Los Angeles. I had found an old family photo dated May 17, 1917, showing me at age six with Mother, an uncle, and assorted others standing at the top of Mt. Rubidoux, a rocky upthrust of nearly eight hundred feet above the Santa Ana River plain. The mountain was topped by a huge wooden cross dedicated to the pioneering Father Junípero Serra. So when we were in nearby Pasadena the winter of 1987–88, seventy years after my first visit and when I had reached 77, I was determined to see this place again.

The upthrust turned out to be in a park but with a one-way, ring-around road to the top. This meant once we had so jauntily started up, there was no turning back. And the road was steep, with no safety rails, in short, a very hairy, scary drive both up and down. We didn't freeze; we couldn't stop; our hearts raced. At the top, one has a sweeping view of the river valley from the small parking area. And above it all stands now a new cross, this one of metal. We found a marker that said President William Howard Taft had been there in 1909. How Taft, who weighed 350 pounds, ever made it, by carriage or early automobile, remains a mystery to me.

I've driven Italy's Amalfi drive, the corniches along France's Riviera, over our own Continental Divide, but Mt. Rubidoux seemed worse. Lois was so scared I told her to close her eyes, but she said she couldn't because I couldn't. Of course, lots of people do drive up Rubidoux, so maybe the experience proved that at 77 one ought to limit his driving to more orthodox roads and highways. Which brings me to the matter of whether one can become too old to drive a car.

One estimate is that there are some 19 million drivers in America who are over 65, about 50 percent more than ten years earlier. Statistics show that the most dangerous drivers, by age groups, are the youngest: under 20 and between 20 and 24. But those drivers 75 and older have more than twice as many accidents as those in the middle brackets, from 45 through 74. In other words, at 80 I'm in a dangerous age group. Increasingly, states are now requiring retesting for license renewal above a certain age. Driver "reeducation" for oldsters has become widespread, indeed a necessity for many.

While I know my reflexes have slowed, so far I have been able to react correctly in unexpected traffic situations. Many of us oldsters take to driving more slowly, to the exasperation of youngsters who seem to think they can blow us off the road with their horns. The 95-year-old father of then vice-presidential candidate Lloyd Bentsen, the Texas senator, was killed when he drove his truck past a stop sign and was hit broadside.

We are reluctant, however, to quit driving; in today's America a car remains a vital link to stores, neighbors, amusements, restaurants—and children and grandchildren. Probably, as the director of Arizona's driver medical-review program was quoted in *Time*, "people age at different rates, so, ideally, it should be done on a case-by-case basis."

But there are compensations to such problems of age. A wonderful thing happened to us in our seventies and continues in our eighties: a particular form of neighborliness. The people who live next door—you should be so lucky—raised and sent off to college four kids, and we got to know them all as a sort of surrogate second generation of our own children.

Somewhere along the line, the parents, Sally and Ainslie Shelburne, a pair of lovely early-to-bed, early-to-rise people, started bringing our morning paper from the circle in front of our driveways, where the *Washington Post* deliveryman tosses it at dawn, right up to our front door, out of reach of rain or snow. It's no fun, you know, to pull boots over slippers and raincoat over bathrobe and to hoist an umbrella to fetch the paper yourself in inclement weather. Besides, it looks ridiculous. One or the other Shelburne walks the dog in the early hours, and so they alibi, "It's no bother."

Can you match that kindness by any of your neighbors? Or by you for a neighbor of yours? It's one of those things that helps one grow old gently.

How Old Is Old?

A DOCTOR WROTE OF visiting a colleague suffering from terminal cancer of the rectum. The victim asked:

"Sam, would you do something for me? Will you please find me the name of the guy who coined the term *golden years*?"

"Why?" the visitor asked.

"I want to give him a good kick in the ass."

Those thirty-something kids on Madison Avenue who write the advertisements have at least learned that people of a certain age think of themselves as fifteen years younger than they really are. Thus it is that we get our backs up at the TV ads for false-teeth stickum, gray-hair eliminators, and all those fiber foods. So, too, we tend to resent such terms as *senior citizens, oldsters,* and *golden years.* The first time I asked at the movies for senior citizen discounts, I cringed, inwardly if not outwardly. So did my wife.

Worse still, the kid in the ticket booth didn't even question my request for senior status. It was insulting. I never thought I looked my age. People told me I didn't, too. If you're 65, you perceive yourself a mere 50; at 80 you kid yourself you're only 65. I know I do, at least on some good days.

Age. I don't know how they can be sure, but they tell us that life expectancy back in the early Iron and Bronze Age Greece was only 20 years; that it moved up to 39 by 1850, and to 48 by the last turn of the century, 1900. In 1910, when I was born, life expectancy for male babies was about 48 and for females around 52. A male born nowadays in America can expect to live 73 years, a female 81. Or, to put it another way, "approximately 80 percent of Americans will live past the age of 65, an age that only one in ten people achieved in earlier generations." Of course, these are overall averages, and we all know there are big differences among racial groups and in the other ways we categorize our population.

HOW DID I GET HERE SO FAST?

The longevity differences between the sexes, however, are narrowing as women, who began smoking later than men, now have rising rates of lung cancer and as younger women, nonsmokers, enter the work force with its often ulcer-producing stresses. Given these facts, it's disheartening to anyone my age to see a clutch of teenage girls puffing away as they eye the opposite sex.

The 1990 census reminds us, if we needed it, how big and growing are the numbers of those of us called older Americans. For a lot of reasons it's been necessary to pin this down in age brackets, and the census people have been doing it this way:

Older	55	through 64
Elderly	65	through 74
Aged	75	through 84
Very old	85	and over

Some gerontologists, however, classify us in a rather simpler way:

Young old	60	through 74
Middle old	75	through 84
Old old	85	and over

Personally, I prefer the second set of terms; I'd rather, at 80, be "middle old" than "aged." It's that business of thinking of yourself as fifteen years younger than you are. But I've come to accept "senior citizen." The term at least has dignity, and it offers some mitigation on bus and subway fares and 10 percent at the pharmacy, as well as at the box office. The movie discount used to pay for the popcorn until the owners got greedy and began sky-highing the food prices.

When I hit 70 and had that big bash, I began to say I was taking life five years at a time. But when I made it to 75, I changed my tune to a year at a time. Now, at 80, I take it a month at a time. No use taking risks. Nobody says "I'm eighty-something."

An article on aging in the Washington Hospital Center's *Centerscope* includes this intriguing paragraph:

"We do know one thing. We are not alone. Aging is a universal phenomenon common to bears and lobsters, trees and men. It is as normal as reproduction, birth, and growth. But perhaps most important for us, it is a process with wide individual variations."

And, the article concludes, in doing

something about our individual longevity "we have far more options than fruit flies." I certainly hope so. I try to see my doctor and my grandchildren regularly. Now I don't mean to overlook my own children, all of whom, as I've already mentioned, are members of the baby boomer generation.

Yet it's been difficult to convince our children that we, my wife and I, are no longer young. Remember the story of my feeding Matthew in the snowstorm when his parents were in Miami at the orchid conference? That was when I was 73. That baby-sitting episode turned out well enough that Matthew's parents began dreaming of attending the next year's conference, this one in Tokyo, for which they had saved up all those frequent-flyer miles.

For the first of what would be many times, I had to come down hard on David, as with Christopher, to get him to believe that Mom and Dad were getting too old for such baby-sitting, or at least such extensive sitting. Dave didn't argue; I just asked, he said. He accepted my reasons. Ever since there's been something of a new look in his eyes, and in his wife's toward Lois and me. Mom and Dad *are* getting older. Certainly one of life's most difficult moments is that instant in which your child or children feel that realization flash across their brains. You grew up thinking Mom and Dad could do anything, were the fount of all knowledge, or at least you grew up accepting some of that.

A while back there was a rather well-contrived, even haunting, scene in a television ad. The product being advertised has long since escaped my memory. But not the ad:

There was husky dad lifting the family canoe off the station wagon roof racks and carrying it over his head down the path to the crystal lake, his boys, perhaps six and eight years old, following along with life jackets and each dragging a paddle in the dirt. Then the scene shifted: the kids are husky baby boomers; together they lift the canoe and carry it off to the lake, one of them handing dad the paddles and saying, "Here, Dad, we'll handle it, you bring the gear." And there was no objection from dad; it was the generational shift.

I don't think Gallup ever took a poll of how much Americans like or liked their grandparents. I was unlucky in that three of my four were dead before I was born. But the fourth, Dad's mother, I remember vividly in a series of mind's-eye vignettes: rustling black taffeta, delicious jams and jellies, the grape arbor behind the old house next to the barn, the crisp, new dollar bill at birthdays and Christmases. Yes, too, the time she popped her false teeth out of her mouth into her hand at her mischievous grandson. It scared the hell out of this nine-year-old, and I must have been obedient for at least a day or so after that. She died, near to 85, when I was still in grade school.

My grandchildren, Lois's and mine, except for Rebecca, who at 13 began a new age of femininity, still seem quite young. That's why signs of growth, mental and physical, are so delightful. Kevin at five answered the phone; and when I asked for his father, Christopher, I heard him turn and call out: "Dad, your dad." Matthew, a year older, was telling Lois something about his father, but instead of describing him as "Dad," he referred to "your son." Growth. It's that kind of thing that makes you want to go on living.

But you can't escape Cicero's rule number two: age "impairs physical vigor." The medics nowadays say that one's strength, stamina, and mobility decreases once you're over 75, and I don't dispute that. One's own attitude toward growing older has a lot to do with how these decreases affect you, of course. An ad for a new magazine called *Longevity* promises to tell you "why pessimists get sick—and old—while optimists don't (sorry, but it's true.)" I agree.

Any one of us who has handled his own children during those "terrible twos," not to mention other ages, knows that a parent— and especially a grandparent—needs plenty of mental alertness and acuteness to cope with youngsters. And you surely need that "physical vigor" to cope with any version of preschoolers. Still, you're smarter than they are, or think you are, so you can anticipate their moves and moods—or try to. But you've got to remember not only where the baby bottles are kept but the after-school pickup schedule, if you're into that sort of baby-sitting.

And of course you have to remember names, especially your children's and grand-children's. Let me tell you about memory.

The writer and editor Bruce Bliven, not too long before he died at 87, produced a charming piece on the foibles of growing old. He said he'd reached that age when the only way he knew whether he'd just done his teeth was to feel the brush. Since then, I've felt the brush myself.

Then there was the predicament of the

bishop of Exeter, as recounted in a biography of actress Nancy Astor. It occurred in England:

"He couldn't find his ticket at the barrier when going for his train. The ticket collector said, 'It doesn't matter.' He said, 'It does matter.' The ticket man said, 'It doesn't.' The bishop said, 'It does because I don't know where I'm going.'"

Well, I'm not that bad, but I sometimes call Kevin Matthew and vice versa, and Lois calls our daughter, Patricia, by the name of one of her sisters, Peggy. Since both our sons married girls named Mary, we have to refer to them, between ourselves, by their maiden names, Fedarko and Higgins. To add to the family confusion, Patricia married a David; we refer to him, again between ourselves, by his last name, Monahan. I've been keeping birthdays, weddings, and anniversaries of note in a little book for many years, and each December when we buy one of those new twelve-month, twelve-page League of Women Voters calendars with a box for each day, I write in red all this vital information. What once was a convenience has become a necessity.

It helps, too, to have a sense of humor. I recently saw on a car in a grocery store lot this bumper sticker: "Of all the things I've lost, I miss my mind most."

Some people are exceptions to this fading-memory business. One was James A. Farley, Franklin Roosevelt's campaign manager and postmaster general. Genial Jim, as they called him, signed in green ink to the joy of Irish Catholic Democrats, knew thousands of constituents by their first names. Such a memory skill is a golden tool for a politician, and Farley could just glance at a face and have the name come instantly to his lips. This skill he retained long after FDR was dead and Farley was making a fortune helping to make Coca-Cola the worldwide product it is today. But the last time I saw him, shortly before his death at 88, the phenomenal memory had finally begun to slip. When I called out the usual "Hello, Jim," a puzzled look replaced his usual grin of recognition. Still, I think his memory and his cheerfulness complemented each other.

Most of us, however, have trouble remembering the name of that last good movie we saw when we want to recommend it to friends, or we've forgotten to enter the last supermarket-check amount and have lost the cash register tab. Or, more seriously, we forget to take this or that pill that the doctor so jauntily prescribed, assuming we'd take it once or twice or thrice a day, whatever he said, and forgetting about our forgettories. The doc probably is too young to be into forgetfulness himself. Routine, I find, is the only answer to these quirks of aging: put the grocery tab in your wallet until you get home, tear out the ad for the movie in the paper, lay out tomorrow's pills before you go to bed tonight.

We all, I imagine, have memory quirks; mine is middle names, and I don't mean such easy ones as Franklin Delano Roosevelt. For instance: the painter who also invented the telegraph is not S.F.B. Morse but Samuel Finley Breese Morse. The architect is Henry Hobson Richardson; the steel baron Henry Clay Frick; the landscape architect Frederick Law Olmsted. And (John) Calvin Coolidge's political mentor, Amherst classmate, and Boston merchant was Frank Waterman Stearns.

Maybe this freak on my part is because of my own odd middle name. It's spelled McGeagh but pronounced McGay, and I've boiled it down to the initial *M*. McGeagh is Scotch-Irish, an American term said to be unknown in Northern Ireland, Protestant Ulster, whence my grandfather McGeagh emigrated. I have to admit to being flabbergasted when each of my sons and their wives gave a son McGeagh for a middle name. I've even written the boys an explanation of its oddity, for them to read when they reach maturity.

However odd McGeagh may be, it has caused me no such problems as my first name has—Chalmers. Now Chalmers is a most peculiar first name because it's also a last name. Most people seem to think it's a last name, and I've been introduced countless times as "Mr. Chalmers." There once was, when I was a boy, a Chalmers automobile. I've had mail addressed to me as Chalmer Robert, Robert Chalmers, C. Roburts, Robert Charmer, Robert Chambers, and recently and in keeping with the Hispanic invasion of America, as Chalmero Roberto. Maybe the funniest of all was a letter I received from a government press agent, a true flak, addressed to Robert Chalmers and beginning "Dear Bob."

Still, by Emerson's law, there are compensations. Very early on in my newspaper career I found that if I called someone on a story and had to leave my name and number for a hoped-for callback, I did far better if I said "Chalmers Roberts" rather than "Mr.

Roberts." Roberts, good Welsh name that it is, is a dime a dozen. I have found only one other Chalmers Roberts. In truth he was christened Henry Chalmers Roberts, but at an early age he had shed the Henry and gone to work for a publisher in London where he became a well-known man-about-town. Somehow we met and he took me to his famous old club, White's. There I saw one ancient member who wore his bowler while eating, a right he alone then had as the last survivor of that day when the decision had been made that for all new members hats at table had finally been ruled out.

This occurred in wartime 1942 when I was working for the U.S. Office of War Information. After I'd spent three weeks as one of the two male U.S. government "escorts" to Eleanor Roosevelt on her tour of Britain, the first lady courteously included our names in her final daily newspaper column about her visit. The other Chalmers Roberts rang me up. His friends, who had read it in the *London Express,* had been sympathizing with him, he explained, on "how tired I must be after following Mrs. R. around. As I only shook her hand warmly on three occasions, I could not make out their meaning. At last it dawned on me—my zany namesake!" Well, I was a lot younger than he. On reflection, then, Chalmers as a first name has its advantages. I've always felt sort of sorry for my fellow journalist, Charles Roberts of *Newsweek;* such an ordinary name. Excuse me, Chuck.

Even though I've spent my working life in journalism where names are vital, I've never been very good at calling them off on sight. Spouses are even more impossible for me. Long ago, therefore, I devised a fudge: a simple gesture toward my wife and the phrase, "Of course, you remember Lois." Any man, short of a dolt, will then mention his wife's name for you.

It's nice to know, too, that sometimes younger people's memories linger over you. Gregory Peck told this story about fellow actor James Mason. Mason was walking in Dublin and heard someone following him. He turned around and saw a young girl. She said: "I was just wanting to see if you really were James Mason—in his later years."

Most of us oldsters can attest to the truth of this Ann Landers column remark: "Older Folks often remember with amazing clarity what happened sixty years ago although they cannot tell you what they ate for breakfast or who visited them yesterday."

Hence I love that doctor who was quoted as saying: "The good news is that unless you're a jet-fighter pilot, the kinds of memory declines that come with growing older don't matter much and can usually be compensated for."

And I like the way a memory specialist at the National Institute of Aging (part of the National Institutes of Health) considers the riddle of differing memory blocks in our brains: "One way to look at it is that those early memories have been there the longest and have been reinforced over the years. Recent stimuli, on the other hand, must compete for space with a lifetime of accumulated data in the brain and have only a short time to be encoded."

Sometimes it feels as though one's head is just stuffed too full of neurons, those brain nerve cells. The system's overloaded and can't take any more. So we slough off the newest data and fall back on that stored long and well in the old nooks and crannies.

Or, as the writer Henry Fairlie, once put it: "In growing old, one has a stocked attic in which to rummage."

Rummage? Yes, sooner or later we all do it, I guess. But before we get to rummaging here—and it's coming, be sure—let's consider being in our eighties and then in our nineties.

Before that, however, a couple of sentences about Fairlie, who died at a mere 66. A colleague's tribute described him this way: "At times he came close to the perfect mix of arbitrary crankiness, occasional wistfulness, and recalcitrant style that is the true art of being old." At least that's the way some youngsters think of us at our best.

On Hitting Eighty

THOMAS G. CORCORAN was a New Deal lawyer, a consummate fixer in matters political, and an accomplished accordion player for President Roosevelt's private parties. Years after FDR had died at only 63, early in his fourth term in the White House, Corcoran was discussing the Roosevelt presidency at a forum. By then Corcoran was into big lawyer-lobbyist money-making and a supporter of Republican president Reagan.

"Now I think Reagan has strengths. He is seventy years old: I am eighty years old. And old age ain't for sissies, even if you are seventy."

It must be about this time in life—one's

eighties—that one comes to agree with "Tommy the Cork," as Roosevelt gaily called him, and disagree with poet Robert Browning. Perhaps you learned these lines as a child, as I did:

Grow old along with me!
The best is yet to be,
The last of life, for which the first was made.

Maybe Browning should be forgiven, though, because he was a mere 52 when he wrote that. I've often wondered if he was reacting to a letter he'd received that same year from fellow poet Walter Savage Landor: "I am nearly blind and totally deaf. My son Charles undresses me, and I do not give any trouble. I dine on soup." Landor was then 89, three weeks from death.

As for Corcoran, he died the year he said "Old age ain't for sissies," at 80. On the other hand, actress Katherine Hepburn embarked on her memoirs at 80, with the comment, "It's later than you think." Maybe that's the line for us 80-year-olds. They say there will be 12 million 80-year-olds by 2010. And the over-85 group is the fastest-growing segment of our population.

Moss Hart, the playwright who died at

only 57, wrote in his delectable *Act One,* a history of his life in the theater, that "time seems to quicken on opening nights and take on a velocity of its own, just as, I imagine, time must seem to hasten for the very old, accelerating with a swiftness imperceptible to the rest of us."

At 55 or so, when he wrote that, Hart may have thought 70 was "very old" or maybe he meant 80. Some in their eighties seem to be waiting to die; I had a brother-in-law who read French literature as he waited patiently. There aren't a lot of us who are charging into our nineties, as did Justice Holmes. I told you I'd get back to him. Here's one story:

At a dinner party when Holmes was 89, he was discussing, with equally elderly friends, a lady of mutual acquaintance. "Holmes asked how she was. Lady Pollock said, 'Well, she's not doing so well. You know she's feeling her years.' Holmes said, 'Really? How old is she?' Lady Pollock said, 'She must be eighty-four or eighty-five.' And Holmes, with this beautiful baritone voice, the light shining on his white hair and mustache, from the head of the table where he was sitting, boomed out, 'Why, what's eighty among adults?'"

Indeed, Holmes at 80 wrote that "I used to think that the main-spring was broken by 80," but now that he had reached that age, "I like it and want to produce as long as I can."

For most of us, however, non-Holmeses, our medicine chests get fuller, our visits to the medics more frequent, our tummies more protrusive, and our wrinkles and crinkles more pervasive, forehead to feet. I'm not even going to mention those who are balding. But why do fingernails and toenails grow so much faster when you're 80? And why is it ever more difficult to file the former and clip the latter? And did the fellow who invented the plastic safety wrappers ever let an 80-year-old try to get one off? Sometimes, too, when you pull off your socks, you wish you had a pair of those shears they use in hospital emergency rooms to separate man from his clothing.

Or, if you catch a sign of aging in the window of a shop as you pass by, you pull yourself up straight, or if your spouse tells you to do so, you pull in your belly, and put the subject out of your mind, if you can. The winter I was 77 we spent in Pasadena, where I was given a pass that allowed me to swim laps in the heated outdoor pools of the California Institute of Technology, Cal

HOW DID I GET HERE SO FAST?

Tech. Sheer joy to shake the bones, not to mention my admiration for, and plenty of envy of, the kids with tight tummy muscles, broad shoulders, or shapely buttocks. Only when I looked in the full-length mirror in the dressing room after showering did I come back to reality; nobody yet has found Ponce de León's fountain of youth, not even Hume Cronyn in the movie *Cocoon*.

Old is physical and mental. The slowing down of a human being is called senility: "mental and physical deterioration with old age," my dictionary says. When you're conscious of this, you don't like the word *senility*. It reminds you too much of friends who have slipped into various forms of mental vacuity. We know, statistically, we're most likely to die of cancer or a heart ailment, but we dread Alzheimer's disease because it robs one of life before one dies.

Senescence is, maybe, a gentler word than *senility*, but its meaning is simply "growing old, aging." We're all senescent, but nobody said it more easily than Ogden Nash:

> *Senescence begins*
> *And middle age ends*
> *The day your descendants*
> *Outnumber your friends.*

A grand example of a person remaining mentally sharp well past the mideighties is George F. Kennan. The diplomat-historian wrote the basic document on the "containment" of Soviet communism back in 1946, and he has lived through the entire Cold War era to see his thesis proved correct. He is still very active, prescribing policy for the post–Cold War age. Or consider Supreme Court Justice William J. Brennan, a liberal among conservatives yet a jurist able to exert vast influence on constitutional law until his retirement at 84.

By our eighties most of us have to make some concessions to the state of our physical health. I'm not talking of those who are still running or playing tennis or doing whatever else is out of the norm for most of us. Prime energy comes in the mornings; make use of it. I wrote most of this between breakfast and lunch, and I had to hold off reading much of the newspaper until later in the day when I tend to feel more tired both physically and mentally.

Some people get by with less sleep as they grow older and therefore are up at dawn and gardening in the dewy hours. Not I. I need my eight, sometimes nine. I am consoled by the words of a Stanford Medical

School professor: "We think that the ability to sleep decreases with age much more than the need to sleep." So I fight my way through the morning distractions to get to my office-at-home and my typewriter. At 80, maybe even at 75, my rule has been, "Don't call me before ten or after nine." Violate it at your peril; I can be worse than merely grumpy.

To keep me working, as on this book, I have posted on the cabinet beside my desk the words of Winston Churchill:

"Writing a book is an adventure. To begin with, it is a toy and an amusement; then it becomes a mistress; then it becomes a master; then it becomes a tyrant. The last phase is that just as you are about to be reconciled to your servitude, you kill the monster and fling him to the public."

Now we oldsters do need exercise, and my regular exercise is swimming, skinny-dipping when we have the pool to ourselves. There's nothing better. One writer rhapsodizes: "One of the sport's main attractions is its Zen of quiet, meditative tranquillity— back and forth, back and forth—that lets the mind float off to peaceful levels of creativity and well-being."

I've always hated calisthenics and all

that, but swimming I love. Every winter is a long wait for spring, unless we can get away to some place in the sun, and every fall is a battle to keep our pool open yet another week. Over the past twenty-five years or so we've managed to have a first swim on or about April 1 and the last as late as election day, the first Tuesday after the first Monday in November. But the glory days for the pool are May through September. April and October are the months you fight with: in the spring, showers of tree blossoms and buds, and in the fall, swirling leaves. At either end of the season all this requires in our part of the country is burning propane gas to heat the water. As you grow older, the cost of the heat grows less important than the heat itself. Then again, I'm more cautious now about those iffy days when I have to decide whether to risk a cold or worse by taking a swim. At 79 I quit taking a running plunge into the pool in favor of a safer dive from the edge. But at 80 I can still pull myself out of the pool by my arms.

The sunshine, and not just incidentally either, feels wonderful. But by the time you're in your seventies, you probably have come to regret so much glorious exposure in your twenties and thirties. We go for an annual skin-cancer checkup at the dermatologist and often he freezes a few spots in time. Have you seen that poster of the marvelously tanned, beautiful young lady under the play-on-words heading "Fry now. Pay later"?

People do get used to being housebound, even wheelchairbound or otherwise physically limited. But none of us has to be told to fight it as long as we can, even if it's only by walking around the block. Older neighborhoods are better than new ones for this; they tend to have sidewalks.

When you boil it all down to the essential, that means keeping your heart pumping, your noodle active, and your mood cheery. One theory is that the best way to stimulate your mind is to receive and absorb a constant supply of new information. Keep the gears moving, so to speak. Don't just read the morning newspaper, turning first, as a lot of us do, to the obituary pages. Get out of the house. Lunch with friends. Go see these movies the young describe as "awesome." Read something that challenges the conventional wisdom in whatever field holds your lifelong interest.

Lots of oldsters travel, and worldwide, too. Cruise ships are fun. We did the Greek isles once and the Hawaiian islands more recently. They do save you the packing and unpacking that different hotels each night require. Some cruises lecture you excessively on what to see next; I always try to do my essential reading before leaving home.

I'm still trying to find out who wrote the words, but I like them, carved into one of the massive panels at the top outside front of Washington's Union Station: "He that would bring home the wealth of the Indies must carry the wealth of the Indies with him. So it is in travelling—a man must carry knowledge with him if he would bring home knowledge."

All these devices help keep the memory sharper. Perhaps someday there will be artificial memory stimulants, a new order of pill popping. Meanwhile, be wary of the pills you're already popping because some pills do adversely affect memory.

Perhaps this is the place to talk about sex. A couple's married life, it turns out, is the foreplay to their retirement life. *Sex After 40* and *Sex After 60* are books written long ago. But *Sex After 80*? Well, if you've come this far and have learned anything, it's that human sexuality—sensual sexuality—is less a matter of age than it is of maturity. That is, mutual sexuality is the enduring kind. So why not *Sex After 80?*

A bitter maxim of La Rochefoucauld: "Old age is a tyrant which forbids, on penalty of death, all the pleasures of youth." I'm not sure exactly what he had in mind, but everybody knows sexual appetites are stronger when you're 20 or 30 than at 70 or 80. Older folks worry about heart attacks; we had a friend who, indeed, "died in the saddle," to use an old expression. Of course, sex at these later ages has a different sense of timing and content, a different mode of agony and ecstasy. This is not a sex guide, so I'll leave it at that. Except for one thing.

And that is to say that January 1948 was one of the truly watershed dates in the twentieth century. Then it was that Alfred C. Kinsey and two associates published their *Sexual Behavior in the Human Male.* With this and their subsequent (1953) study on female sexuality, Kinsey shattered the then seemingly pervasive Victorian conventions and strictures in America. It seems to me that the orgiastic extremes of the sexual revolution of the 1960s and 1970s were a reaction against the long history of sexual repression in the Western world, especially in America.

As a Princeton sociologist has put it,

pre-Kinsey "the official version emphasized marriage, sex in marriage and only rarely for pleasure." Or as a book reviewer wrote: "One of the most miraculous things about evolution is that it has built into both sexes the capacity not just for passion or romance but for lasting love."

Isn't this what makes *Sex After 80* possible? I don't want to make a federal case out of the idea that sex can continue until you drop at 100. I only want to say that sex for pleasure is a healthy and satisfying component of life as long as it is physically possible. Hedley Donovan, the former head of Time Inc., put it simply: "God has arranged for it to be fun."

That includes a lot more than orgasms. If you don't already know, haven't long experienced, the sexuality of sleeping together naked under an electric blanket, you've missed a lot in life. Or swimming naked, as I've already mentioned. Those who have never felt their whole bodies awash in river, lake, sea, or pool haven't really lived.

Those among us now in their eighties tend to have been a working male and a housekeeping and child-raising female, a vanishing breed nowadays. (Of our three children, one fits that description; the other two have job-holding spouses.)

HOW DID I GET HERE SO FAST?

In our case, Lois and I were ahead of our time; we both always worked. I was a journalist, she, as I mentioned earlier, a small bookstore owner-proprietor for thirty-one years. The day I retired she sold the bookstore. My wife is a grand gardener (speciality: daylilies), a sometime painter, she's always in the middle of several books at once. We can't do all we used to; travel has become harder. Tapering off while still enjoying is the key. Still, it's hard to give up a favorite flower bed (or my red raspberry patch) or to pass up visiting some spot you missed, or saw and loved, on earlier trips.

Given the fact that about half of American marriages nowadays end in divorce, couples heading toward their fiftieth wedding anniversaries are either living together for convenience or they have made the necessary adjustments to make their marriage work. We can, or at least we used to be able to, work up a storm over how our books are put on the shelves. She alphabetizes by authors; I cluster by subject and era. Her shelves are loaded with fiction; mine with nonfiction. Every now and then one does get the other to read something one truly likes; often it's a time-saver to share the best parts by reading out loud to your spouse this bit or that.

Of course married couples have to work out compromises; there is no perfect yin and yang in marriage. So you decide who does what chores, the bill paying, grocery shopping, cooking, loading the dishwasher, taking out the trash, you name it. Probably the most successful material thing we ever did for married harmony was to put two sinks in our bathroom.

We all have our idiosyncrasies. If you have that feeling, as I do, that you want to get to bed when your partner does, then you'll have to compromise. I always seem to have one more thing to read—occasionally, one more bit of TV to see—when she's ready "to go up." So we haggle-paggle over the last fifteen minutes or so.

About half of Americans age 70 and over say they eat out at least once a week. It is a way to escape some of the chores of householding as well as to keep up with the changing scene all about you. We try to eat lunches out with special friends, Dutch treat, from time to time. Even though entertaining at home becomes more burdensome, there are now available lots of good take-home dishes one can serve guests. And I can still get a cork out of a wine bottle.

Restaurants change rapidly; it's a high-risk business. But there are always new ones to try and some of the oldies are still golden, both as to food and ambiance.

A truly sad scene is a couple sitting silent in a restaurant, apparently having exhausted life's conversation. It's depressing; try to avoid places like that. Try a place where parents bring kids; they're noisy, but you'll quickly be recalling how you, too, struggled through a meal with the kids squirming down from their chairs and scattering through the aisles. You relive this scene even more dramatically when you take out your children and their children.

Do you remember how much faster your children used to eat than you did? Or have you noticed that now that your children are parents, they gobble up their food almost as fast as their kids, your grandchildren? I ascribe this latter phenomenon to the arrival of the fast-food business, not just to the siren call of television as a counterattraction to family-table conversation. It takes a heap of discipline to keep them at the table nowadays.

At a restaurant it's terrible to see a couple talking past each other, neither listening. When we see such a couple, or a silent pair, we like to play the guessing game: Who are they, what do—did—they do; why so silent or gabby? Watch their body language; it tells a lot. Some wives drive husbands into silence. Moss Hart recalled that "the simple fact was that my father had grown increasingly lonely as his role in the family circle grew dimmer and as my mother's dominant personality gradually rubbed out his own more gentle one." Only occasionally do you see it the other way around.

A *Los Angeles Times* columnist invented, I think, the word duologue to describe a conversation in which neither party is responsive to the other. Maybe he thought duologue was endemic to Hollywood; we've found it worldwide. It's awful. But it's nothing new. Grandmas used to talk about people who were "sot" in their ways. I guess those grandmas would have applied that term to Archie Bunker's attitude about his chair.

There are, however, sexual differences in the approach to conversation. Consider this analysis from Deborah Tannen, a professor of linguistics, as printed in the *Washington Post:*

"When a woman tells about a problem, instead of saying he understands and offering a similar problem, a man is likely to offer a solution. Such an instrumental approach is like a wrench thrown into the conversation works. If matching troubles frames two people as similar and equal, offering a solution frames the problem solver as one-up. The hierarchical distinction is distancing, just the opposite of the sought-for rapport. Furthermore, a man who thinks telling problems is a request for advice expects his solution to be adopted, or at least considered, but solutions are irrelevant to women looking for understanding. The man ends up frustrated: she complains but doesn't want to do anything to solve her problems."

Worst of all, in my experience, is the couple who bicker in public. They have no business inflicting on others their unhappiness, whether it's over who's to change the baby, why there isn't more money, or who made what wrong remark at what party. I suppose that one spouse thinks she/he is punishing the other by doing so in front of others, be they relatives or only passing acquaintances. But the blind can't see, and this is just one reason why the American family today is so divorce prone. Columnist David Broder wrote that this larger problem has grown so that many have a "feeling the social fabric is being torn apart." I haven't mentioned alcohol or drugs.

Those of us who are still married at 80 come from the old stability. If man and wife have survived this far in reasonable, even passable, livable health, divorce is not in their future. Just don't bicker, quarrel, natter, picky-pick in public, please.

At older ages kisses may not inflame as they once did, but they come to mean very, very much. They are the affirmation of the bonds that have held two people together so long. They seal those timeless words "I just need love" and "I love you."

Picket-Guard
at Ninety

W E HAVE FRIENDS IN
their nineties, some in better shape than
others, some still throwing dinner parties,
others invalided by strokes. In a sense, they
all are our "picket-guards." Let me explain.

Justice Holmes's father, Oliver Wendell
Holmes, Sr., was a Boston physician who
became instantly famous at twenty-one when
he dashed off a stirring patriotic poem to
help prevent the breakup of the USS *Constitution*. She was the most famous ship of the
War of 1812, a frigate known as *Old Ironsides*,
which you can visit today in Boston harbor.
Part of his poem goes like this:

Ay! pull her tattered ensign down,
  Long has it waved on high,
And many a heart has danced to see
  That banner in the sky. . . .

Oh better that her shattered hulk
  Should sink beneath the wave;
Her thunders shook the mighty deep
  And there should be her grave;
Nail to the mast her holy flag.
  Set every threadbare sail,
And give her to the God of storms—
  The lightning and the gale!

Dr. Holmes went on to combine writing and medicine with great success, becoming known, from the title of a series of his essays, as "the autocrat of the breakfast table." In 1867, when his son was a 26-year-old beginning lawyer, the senior Holmes turned out a novel called *The Guardian Angel.* Though not yet 60, the doctor gave the term *picket-guard,* used in the just-ended Civil War, a new meaning in this perceptive passage about those in their nineties:

"A man over ninety is a great comfort to all his elderly neighbors: he is a picket-guard at the extreme outpost; and the young folks of sixty and seventy feel that the enemy must get by him before he can come near their camp."

That's the way, in your eighties, you'll likely be feeling about your elders who've already hit 90. At least I do. The notion keeps you going. It keeps you from having the creeps when you see in your college alumni magazine that the notes for your class keep moving closer and closer to the front. Thank God for those "picket-guards."

Maybe you baby boomers will be heartened to know that there are some 75 million of us Americans older than you—your "picket-guards." That's a substantial buffer, for now anyway.

Oliver Wendell Holmes, Jr., carried into his nineties something besides his good genes: a joie de vivre that showed itself at an early age and never left him. This was quite obvious in his attitude toward, indeed his relationships with, women. It is the focus of a marvelous account of Holmes's "mellow years" by John S. Monagan in his *The Grand Panjandrum*.

Holmes and his wife, Fanny—she died at 88—were a devoted, childless couple. Early on she had realized her husband had a roving eye for the opposite sex. Fanny Holmes, however, was not just the wife who subordinated her life to that of her husband, although she saw to his comfort, his privacy, his switch from horse and carriage to automobile. She was a woman of wit and substance. Her best-known bon mot was uttered at President Theodore Roosevelt's White House dinner table:

"Washington is full of famous men and the women they married when they were young."

As Holmes became a figure of national and international reputation, Fanny took a live-and-let-live attitude toward him and his lady friends. During Supreme Court summer recesses, she encouraged him to travel solo to England and Ireland. There he had what Monagan describes as a "long and fervid relationship" with a married, and titled, Englishwoman, beginning when he was 55 and she 43. He burned her letters but she saved his.

A "fervid relationship" then was far more discreet than now, so perhaps we should not let our imaginations run too far and fast. There is, however, plenty of evidence that Holmes liked and attracted women and that they were attracted to him. To a friend he said: "One of my greatest problems is to find available vices for old age."

In Paris, Holmes took in the Folies-Bergère; Fanny was along on that trip but managed that evening to be indisposed. Later on, in Washington, he began to turn up regularly on Friday evenings at the now long-gone Gayety burlesque theater on seedy Ninth Street where he enjoyed the stripteasers. A fellow Gayety attendee quoted him: "Thank God, I've got low tastes."

During Holmes's walks with his various law secretaries (today, at the Supreme Court, they're called law clerks), he exercised that eye for the women. One clerk, when Holmes was in his eighties, reported that the justice "would look them all over up and down, and if they were young and beautiful, he would comment with the appreciation of a connoisseur upon the particular feature of beauty, whatever it was, all the way from the ankles to the hair."

His clerk during Holmes's last year on the court described the Holmes method as it was applied to the clerk's own wife and in his presence:

"I feel temperate when I say of the Justice that he was always willing to make a favorable impression upon a new bird of the opposite sex. He fixed her attention. Then a steady stream of the deepest philosophy poured from his lips. The beautiful sonorous voice flowed on. The listener tried to conceal her panic and the agony with which she was striving to have an intelligent comment ready at the peroration."

In this particular case, however, Holmes's wife also was present, and "at the critical zenith" of her husband's words to the young lady, Fanny's "phrase shot out like a needle against a balloon: 'George! [by George] You do talk pretty.'"

Holmes was 90 at the time. At 80 he had written: "It seems as if a man must reach 90 to be really old. But I guess it is pretty hard sledding to get there." Yes; true. But when he got there, his zest seemed undiminished. The summer he was 91, and back vacationing at his Beverly Farms in Massachusetts, lots of old friends came to visit, bringing along the young he so much enjoyed. In her *Yankee from Olympus*, Catherine Drinker Bowen drew this charming scene:

"Sitting on the porch he discussed life with Betsy Warder, aged sixteen. 'I won't refrain from talking about anything because you're too young,' Holmes told her, 'if you won't because I'm too old.'"

Perhaps it was about this time that Holmes wrote a friend, as quoted in Sheldon M. Novick's admirable biography, that "it is not only that grandmothers are younger and bottles smaller than once, but years are oh so much shorter."

Agnes Meyer recounted visiting the

widowed Holmes at his I Street house and finding him reading Aristotle's "Grammar." When she asked, "Why are you wasting time on that dry stuff?" Holmes "replied with twinkling eyes, 'I am preparing for my last examination.'"

The Civil War, in which Holmes was thrice wounded—at Ball's Bluff, at Antietam, and near Chancellorsville—permeated the rest of his life: his language, his personal actions, beliefs, judicial decisions. Donald Hiss, who served the just-retired justice in 1932–33, recalled driving with Holmes "everywhere from Fort Sumner down to Mt. Vernon." That is, they visited all the remnants of the Civil War forts thrown up early in the conflict to protect the capital city from the rebels camped just south of the Potomac, with Washington's home south of the last fort as an extra attraction for Holmes.

Long associated with Holmes, although of doubtful authenticity, is the famous story of President Lincoln at Fort Stevens, one of those forts and the only one to come under fire from Confederate forces. Holmes, as a young lieutenant, undoubtedly was there, and probably there when the President rode out from the White House to see what rebel raider Jubal Early and his troops were up to.

Lincoln, complete with tall stovepipe hat, stood up on the ramparts, the better to observe, just as a Union officer standing nearby fell to a sharpshooter's bullet. At this Holmes cried out: "Get down, you damn fool, or you'll get shot."

James H. Rowe, Holmes's last clerk, heard Holmes tell the tale, as did at least one other clerk, but Rowe considered it apocryphal. Everybody liked it so much, however, they kept on telling it. At Fort Stevens today there is a bronze plaque on the parapet that shows young Holmes tugging at Lincoln's arm as the officer falls next to him. Rowe also told this story: Holmes thrust out his hand to his clerk and said: "Sonny, shake the hand of a man who shook the hand of a Revolutionary War soldier."

Two more Holmes stories of his nineties, the first about his ninetieth birthday, the second about the call the newly inaugurated president, Franklin D. Roosevelt, made at Holmes's house when he became 92.

On his ninetieth birthday, Sunday, March 8, 1931, there were many greetings and salutations for the world-famous justice. A national radio hookup connected Holmes's study with friends gathered in Boston and in New York. After the preliminaries, the congratulations, the long-life wishes, the reminiscences, came Holmes himself. His message:

> In this symposium my part is only to sit in silence. To express one's feelings as the end draws near is too intimate a task.
>
> But I may mention one thought that comes to me as a listener-in. The riders in a race do not stop short when they reach the goal. There is a little finishing canter before coming to a standstill. There is time to hear the kind voices of friends and to say to one's self: "The work is done." But just as one says that, the answer comes: "The race is over, but the work is never done while the power to work remains." The canter that brings you to a standstill need not be only coming to rest. It cannot be while you still live. For to live is to function. That is all there is to living.
>
> And so I end with a line from a Latin poet who uttered the message more than fifteen hundred years ago:
>
> "Death plucks my ear and says, Live—I am coming."

Less than a year later, declining health caused Holmes to resign from the Court. But there was to be one more finale. On Holmes's ninety-second birthday, March 8, 1933, only four days after FDR had been sworn in as president for the first time, Roosevelt came to Holmes's small town house at 1720 I Street Northwest (now given way to a glossy office building).

Felix Frankfurter had set up the visit, and Donald Hiss bought champagne from a bootlegger (it still was the era of Prohibition) for a luncheon party with Corcoran and others.

The following paragraphs comprise Hiss's account in Katie Louchheim's *The Making of the New Deal: The Insiders Speak:*

We didn't take our drive that day. The streets were crowded, and it was not a very pleasant day. I didn't want Holmes to get too tired. I had read to him, but he had nodded off to sleep. I kept going back and forth between the library on the second floor and the bedroom where he slept to be sure that we knew when the President arrived, because Holmes was then in his old alpaca coat. When I saw the open car drive up and a crowd gathering immediately, I said, "Mr. Justice, I think the President of the United States is outside." He woke up and said, "Don't be an idiot, boy. He wouldn't call on me." And I said, "I'm pretty sure it is." "Well, we'd better not take any chances. Give me your arm. Get this coat off." So I got his alpaca coat off and got him into his swallowtail coat. Then the doorbell rang and I said. "It is the President. He's coming up."

FDR's wheelchair just fit into the elevator Mrs. Holmes had had installed for her husband's use. Soon the president, Mrs. Roosevelt, son James Roosevelt, and Frankfurter were seated in the library. Hiss "just hovered to see if I could be of any assistance." There ensued one of the great, if unintended, putdowns of American history. Their age difference of forty-two years allowed the old justice to reach further back, indeed to America's pre-independence era. Here is Hiss's account:

The conversation was very animated. Holmes had a pair of swords, which his grandfather, Charles Jackson, had used in the Indian wars; they hung over the fireplace. The President noted that they were very handsome. Holmes told him that they were his grandfather Jackson's, who later went on the Massachusetts Supreme Court of Appeals. Holmes then remarked. "I remember that my governor [an upper-class Briticism for one's father] told me that he was having lunch as a young student and his father came home for lunch, as he frequently did, with a friend. And the friend said, "You know, I saw that little West Indian bastard downtown today," referring of course to Alexander Hamilton. Holmes added, "That takes us way back to Alexander Hamilton." The President remarked, "Well, my grandmother goes back as far as the Revolutionary War, but not as far as the Indian wars."

After some further conversation and as FDR prepared to leave, he asked Holmes: "Have you got any final advice for me?" Holmes: "No, Mr. President. The time I was in retreat, the Army was in retreat in disaster, the thing to do was to stop the retreat, blow your trumpet, have them give the order to charge. And that's exactly what you are doing. This is the admirable thing to do and the only thing you could have done."

Hiss recounted that after FDR was gone, Holmes said to him: "You know, I haven't seen Frank Roosevelt for years, but this ordeal of his with polio, and also the governorship and the presidency, have made his face much stronger than it was when I knew him, when he was Assistant Secretary of the Navy during the [first world] war."

Holmes's opinion of President Theodore Roosevelt, who had appointed him to the Court in 1902, is equally fascinating, not to mention TR's opinion of Holmes after the justice dissented from a decision Roosevelt favored. Said TR: "I could carve out of a banana a judge with more backbone than that."

With more hindsight, Holmes drew this cameo of TR: "He was very likable, a big figure, a rather ordinary intellect, with extraordinary gifts, a shrewd and I think pretty unscrupulous politician. He played all his cards—if not more."

What is it about those men and women who make it into their nineties? Good genes, mostly, no doubt, but also their attitude toward life. Muckraking journalist George Seldes published his fascinating autobiography at 96. Industrialist Armand Hammer's ego as well as his industry kept him humming to 92. William Paley, founder of the CBS network, who died at 89, never quit working there. Or consider Eleanor Lansing Dulles's enthusiastic infatuation at 95 with postwar Germany and Berlin. Jay Gorney, who made it to 93, wrote the music for the song of the Great Depression, "Brother, Can You Spare a Dime?" Alice Roosevelt Longworth, TR's daughter, who lived to 96, made a career of being an iconoclast. Although she was credited, and delightedly so, with having characterized GOP presidential candidate Thomas E. Dewey as looking "like the little man on the wedding cake," she told me she had heard that one from her dentist. She also regaled me, when she was 90, with her account of FDR's romance during the First World War with his wife's, Eleanor's, secretary, Lucy Mercer. Alice recounted that FDR had brought the "slim and attractive" Lucy to dine at her house a couple of times after Eleanor had taken the Roosevelt children off to Campobello for the summer. And Alice added that she teased Roosevelt after seeing him driving Lucy about town: "Franklin, that was a lovely girl," to which he smilingly responded: "Isn't she."

Some among us will make it all the way through the nineties to their centennial year. For me, that's too far. I just couldn't face those centenarian newspaper interviews. How did you do it? asks, usually, some young whippersnapper who's barely shaved or just graduated from Stanford or Bryn Mawr and who's been sent out on a first interviewing assignment. A tot of whiskey every night before bed, was it? (Old people, these kids think, need to be led into answers.) Absolutely no alcohol, you say? Rhubarb pie you baked yourself, eh? Drink lots of fresh milk? Don't these young people know about dairy products and cholesterol?

(After I'd written that last paragraph, believe it or not, I came upon the obituary of one John Evans, a Welsh coal miner, who died at 112 and who had made it into the *Guinness Book of World Records* as the world's oldest man. Listen: "He attributed his longevity to not drinking, smoking, swearing, or gambling, and to drinking a concoction of honey and hot water each morning."!!)

Irving Berlin lived to be 101, but his last years were anything but happy. America's great songwriter was full of "vituperative behavior," self-torment, and fear of being forgotten. As book reviewer Jonathan Yardley put it:

"Extended life may be a blessing but surely a mixed one. Living beyond one's time, beyond the duration of one's powers, can be a curse; certainly it seems to have been Irving Berlin's."

My personal target is my ninetieth year—the Big Two, 2000. I've already written in *Smithsonian* magazine about the dispute between the purists, who insist that the twenty-first century and the third millennium begin on January 1, 2001, and the sentimentalists, who choose January 1, 2000. I'm for the early birds. If I make it to then, I'll have outlived every single one of my ancestors of whom I have an age record, including my favorite. He was great-great-grandfather Hugh Roberts, who came from Wales and made it to 87.

Hugh Roberts's tombstone bears only his name and dates. I prefer those with a bit of zip:

She drank good ale, good punch, and wine
And lived to the age of 99.

Or even:

Been Here
And Gone
Had a Good Time.

Mystic Chords of Memory

HENRY FAIRLIE, WHOM I quoted a while back as saying that "in growing old, one has a stocked attic in which to rummage," went on to add, "and the still-passing show and pageant of life to observe, not only at a more leisurely pace, but with the convincing satisfaction and interest of having lived through many of the changes, even from their beginnings, that have brought us from there to here."

That's certainly true, for example, of the Cold War. For anybody of, say, 60 or over the Cold War was a chilling reality that induced a whole range of emotions from sheer terror of a sudden Pearl Harbor–type nuclear attack on our heads to such fear and panic that some among us even departed the United States for a distant island refuge. The point is simply that we who survived did live through it all, 1945–1990. What comes after may not be all that grand and glorious either—democracy is usually quite untidy and has a lot of raw edges—but the feeling of relief at the end of the Cold War, for those who remember all or most of those four and a half decades, is surely one of the great human emotions of any lifetime.

But to go back to Fairlie's quote about observing the "still-passing show . . . at a more leisurely pace." That's too slow for me. Sure, I'm still an old firehorse of a reporter, greedily reading every word of today's post–Cold War news. I also try to keep in contact with it and not just through watching the tube. I mean Lois and I go to talks, lectures, movies, shows, and such, and we do swap lots of talk with old friends.

When you retire, you soon find out who were your friends and who were the friends of the organization you worked for. In my case, I never had any illusion that it was because of my bright blue eyes that I got invited to all those insider meetings with bigwigs here and abroad and to all those fancy embassy dinners. It was because I carried the imprimatur of my employer, the important, and powerful, *Washington Post.* A lot of those "friends" vanished soon after I retired, but a surprisingly pleasing number have continued to spend time with us these many years.

Indeed, among those you knew in the old days who were younger than you, the truly lovely people are those who don't forget you when you're past, say, 75; for example, the couples who invite you to their parties or the fellow who asks you to lunch or the club even though, by your numerical age, you may seem to be a has-been or an over-the-hiller compared to their other friends.

Just as we try to keep up-to-date, try to keep looking forward in this so fascinating world, we oldsters, admittedly, also do a lot of looking back. We are bonded to the past by our children as well as to the future by our grandchildren. As Dr. Arthur Kornhaber put it, "There's much more to being a grandparent than the biblical continuity of begot, begot, and begot." But aging goes even further than that. Fairlie was right that we do have "a stocked attic in which to rummage."

So let us examine "the mystic chords of memory." It is one of my favorite phrases, crafted as you may know, by Abraham Lincoln for his first inaugural address. He was elected on November 6, 1860, but by the time he reached Washington for the inauguration the following March 4, seven states had already seceded from the Union and had set up the Confederate States of America. Lincoln thus began as a save-the-Union president (the abolishing-slavery president came later), and it was with this in mind that he drafted his first inaugural address. At that time the first shots had not yet been fired at Fort Sumter; saving the Union might still be possible.

So what he had to say that March 4 included this:

"The mystic chords of memory, stretching from every battlefield, and patriot grave, to every living heart and hearthstone, all over this broad land, will yet swell the chorus of the Union, when again touched, as surely they will be, by the better angels of our nature."

Remember, Lincoln was talking to people about the American Revolution, a handful of whose veterans still lived. The day he spoke was almost exactly midway between the British surrender at Yorktown in 1781 and the Japanese attack on Pearl Harbor in 1941. And that attack was only half a century ago. So short are America's two-plus centuries of history as a nation.

Lincoln's appeal to those "mystic chords" failed to keep the states together, and our bloodiest war ensued. Because he was assassinated at the moment of military victory, he became an almost sanctified figure to much of the nation. If you walk past the Lincoln Memorial in Washington in the evening, with only the lights flooding down on Daniel Chester French's brooding statue, and you don't get goose pimples, something's wrong: you haven't caught the American spirit, or you haven't learned American history.

When I was a teenager in Pittsburgh, memorizing the Gettysburg Address and beginning to learn something of my ancestors, I discovered that I had one of those "mystic chords" that somehow, however faint the tie, link one generation to another. These are the very fibers of the shared memories of all cultures, whether passed down as tales, folklore, song, ballad, or in print, or in today's world by oral history on tape as well as on film with sound.

My "mystic" tie to Lincoln was Emily Roberts, an aunt who died when I was three. Four days past her twenty-seventh birthday, my dad assured me, she made her way to Gettysburg for the cemetery dedication, a train trip across nearly half of Pennsylvania. But if she was impressed by his words, indeed if she could get close enough, and soon enough, to hear those few but glorious sentences, she left no record. Nor did her printed obituary mention it. Which makes me wonder if it is just one of those family tales that we want to believe.

The story is a strong reminder of how fleetingly we let our history pass by. How often have you said to yourself or to your spouse: I must put down Grandpa's account of his wartime experiences; I must ask Grandma how her father came to America and what he told her about the old country and his upbringing there? Or how about Dad's experience during World War II, Korea, or Vietnam—or the Great Depression? Or about Mom's wartime experiences on the home front?

I guess it's my reportorial training that spurs me to write those stories down, so I have collected a lot of family histories just in case my children, perhaps even their children, may someday wonder about their ancestors. I don't consider this to be ancestor worship or *Mayflower* madness, just "mystic chords of memory" such as you, the reader, must have regardless of what corner of the globe your ancestors left to come to America. We are all immigrants, or their descendants, as FDR once teasingly told a startled convention of the Daughters of the American Revolution. Each must search out his own "mystic chords," which is what makes it so much fun and can give so much delight.

Who, for example, can excel the story told me by a teenage waiter in a Vietnamese restaurant? He crossed the South China Sea in an overloaded boat, helped fight off pirates, saw many of his companions slain, almost died himself as one boat tipped over. Yet he knew where he came from, who his family was and what they had accomplished, and he declared that he was now more of a believer in God than ever before in his short life. Passage to Ellis Island hasn't been the only entry, the only Golden Door.

Anytime, however, you are seriously dipping into genealogical research and you feel a bit of pomposity coming on—say you've just found a possible ancestral tie to someone famous—here's the perfect way to deflate. Go to your public library and get out *The Norman Rockwell Album,* a portfolio of his drawings, and look on page 175. One of his old *Saturday Evening Post* covers, reproduced there in color, is "A Family Tree." It's not only a splendid sample of the master illustrator's work but hilarious as well, for he was kidding those who worship ancestors. On top of the tree he drew is the all-American boy, circa the 1950s; below are all his ancestors, and they're not just upright American couples, including Union and Confederate veterans. There's a rough, tough old Indian fighter and his squaw, and eight generations back a ferocious, eye-patched pirate and his senorita from the Spanish Main, along with a suggestive half-buried treasure trove and a burning, probably looted, galleon.

Many of those among us who are WASPs (White, Anglo-Saxon, Protestant) can trace our genealogy back a good many generations, but that's not true for many of those whose ancestors came from lands other than Western Europe. Of our two daughters-in-law, one's family tree has been carefully compiled back to at least England in 1643, while the other's trace seems quickly lost in the fragments of Czarist Russia and the Austro-Hungarian Empire. Yet who's to doubt they both must be full of fascinating, as well as ordinary, folk?

It's worth noting, too, that the current surge in immigration in America, legal and illegal, may upset some of the population projections because of the many young people and children involved. Also, it's changing America's racial complexion.

Sen. Daniel Patrick Moynihan has predicted that early in the twenty-first century the American people will be markedly brown, Spanish-speaking, young, and Catholic. We shall see before long if he's right. At any rate, George Herbert Walker Bush is such an outstanding example of a WASP that, in a sense, he may be masking the change envisioned by Moynihan.

Already in California what are now called "non-Hispanic whites" have become the minority in the state's public schools. In California these "Anglos" (for Anglo-Saxons) are being outnumbered by the sum total of Hispanics (also called Latinos), Asians, and blacks (or African Americans).

This kind of fact is hard for some among us to take, those who pridefully think of themselves as "native-born white Americans." One such lady complained in a letter to the editor: "I can only wonder who coined such a babblespeak phrase [as 'non-Hispanic white,'] and how I became a negative without knowing it."

Well, I'm a WASP and so was great-great-grandpa Roberts, who built himself a still-standing log cabin in the western-Pennsylvania wilderness way back in 1799. To have felt, as I have, his adz marks on the massive chestnut logs he felled was to have established a mystic chord of memory, indeed.

Hugh Roberts emigrated from north Wales, probably in 1784, and he came from a lovely little town named Bala that my wife and I have visited. He started out with a young wife, who took sick and died on the way across the Atlantic. I imagine her being buried at sea. During her illness an even younger woman, 15 or 16, helped take care of her; in time she became the second Mrs. Roberts and my great-great-grandmother. What's interesting about her is that she came from Brittany, across the English Channel in France, the last British toehold on the continent. This girl was crossing the Atlantic with her older brother; their names were Elizabeth and Robert Roderique, so it says on their tombstones in Ebensburg, Pennsylvania. Their Anglicized first names suggest their family's movement from France to England at a time unfathomable.

But to get back to Lincoln and those "mystic chords." My wife was born in Washington, D.C., and one of her Unitarian Sunday-school teachers was Miss Helen Nicolay, daughter of one of Lincoln's two personal secretaries, John Nicolay. I first visited Washington with Dad during World War I and came to work in 1933, the first year of FDR's New Deal. So it would have been hard to escape Lincoln. The Ford's Theater box where he was sitting when he was fatally shot, the derringer that did the deed, the house across the street where he died, the Lincoln bed in the White House (a replica of which is now enshrined in, of all places, Richard Nixon's presidential library-museum in California), Fort Stevens where Holmes saw him under fire. On and on it goes.

Mathew Brady, the famous Civil War photographer, used a youthful nephew, Levin Handy, as his apprentice. Handy later had two daughters, who, by the time I met them in 1947 or 1948, must have been well into their seventies. Since I then was in my thirties, they seemed rather antique. But in their long-gone little old brick house on

Maryland Avenue, almost across the street from today's massive Air and Space Museum, I discovered that Mrs. Mary Handy Evans and Mrs. Alice Handy Cox, both then widows, had a treasure trove.

Passed down from their father, who had somehow obtained them from Brady and from his assistant photographers, were a large number of original glass-plate negatives. The largest of these cumbersome and fragile plates were twelve by fifteen inches; many had sustained damage over the intervening decades, including some with cracked glass. When I saw the first Lincoln portrait among them, the portrait reproduced by engraving for the five-dollar bill, I felt like Howard Carter on first entering King Tut's tomb. The Handy daughters sold me original prints from two negatives, the Lincoln five-dollar and Brady's first (circa 1861) photograph of the White House. Both now hang framed on our walls. And both bear the Handy daughters' red stamp: "L. C. Handy Studios, 494 Maryland Ave. S. W., Washington, D.C. Successor to Mathew Brady, the oldest commercial studios in the United States."

At the time I was doing a picture history of Washington, so I often visited the two ladies. One day when I walked in, one of them said, "Come here, Mr. Roberts, we think we've discovered something interesting. What do you think this is?" She held up a glass-plate negative, a portrait of a woman wearing a turban around her hair. "We think," she said, since I was obviously an ignoramus, "this is the first photograph ever found of Dolley Madison." Indeed, it so proved to be. Dolley was the first lady not only for her husband, James Madison (1809–17), but also for the widowed Thomas Jefferson, his predecessor (1801–9), while Madison was his secretary of state. Fortunately, all these precious negatives ended up in the Library of Congress's Brady-Handy Collection.

Finally, to finish this Civil War and Lincoln "mystic chords" business, there are two of our grandfathers. Both Union, but how different their stories. My grandpa Chalmers Thomas Roberts (1834–1909) died the year before I was born, so as a child I used to see on his grave the metal emblem of the Grand Army of the Republic with its small American flag and the fresh-cut family flowers. He was an original Republican, quoted in a newspaper as saying: "I am stronger than ever in my faith in the Grand Old Party.

My first vote for president was for the Pathfinder [John C. Frémont, the GOP's first candidate, in 1856]. I have never missed an election since, and I hope to be spared to cast a vote for President Roosevelt." He was, and that would be Theodore Roosevelt in 1904. Doubtless, too, he voted in 1908 for Republican Taft.

But Grandpa's Civil War record was close to zero. I'm not even sure he didn't buy a "substitute" to take his place, as a lot of Northern sunshine patriots did. He did enlist in a local Cambria County company of the Pennsylvania militia, but the unit saw active duty only once. The governor called it up, along with other units, when Lee's army invaded Maryland in 1862, threatening to cross into Pennsylvania. The troops were used as a backup for the Army of the Potomac, but saw no action in the battle that ensued, known as Antietam to the North, Sharpsburg to the South, and indisputably including the bloodiest single day of the war. From then on Grandpa Roberts rested on his laurels.

My wife's grandpa Hall was cut from a different Union cloth. He was one of the original young and reckless. George Hemingway Birtby Hall (1843–1928) ran away from home at 15, finally joined up at 18 as a self-described "dog robber," a sort of handyman or gofer for officers, in a Michigan outfit. He enlisted under a false name, apparently to hide from his parents, fought from the First Bull Run, enlisting and reenlisting, marched through Georgia under Sherman, made it to Appomattox, and participated in the subsequent Grand Review on Pennsylvania Avenue. Perhaps the high point of his life, at least to me the finest of his mystic chords, came on July 11, 1864. Confederate general Jubal Early had swept down on the capital city from the north, invading the District of Columbia and reaching Fort Stevens, the place where Wendell Holmes saw Lincoln under fire.

Grandpa Hall wrote that "the fight itself was a mere skirmish and was close to town, and I heard it myself from [the] Seventh Street wharf where with my regiment we had just landed from New Orleans." Private Hall's current enlistment then was up, and like many others in the regiment he was figuring to move on. But President Lincoln, he recounted, came down to the wharf, urged the men to sign up again and join the fresh forces being rushed out to Fort Stevens. Grandpa did; but the shooting was soon over, and he never got involved in that skirmish.

One more Lincoln story. In the fall of 1935, a pal, Alfred Friendly, and I were riding a freight train in Illinois, part of a year's travels around the country to discover America. The Great Depression was still very much with us, economically speaking, although in the two and a half years FDR had now been president, he had turned around the national mood from despair to hope. As the freight we were riding approached Springfield, several of the other "knights of the road," as the free riders were sometimes called, advised me and my pal how to flip a freight. They warned us to get off quickly as we pulled into the railroad yards; if we dallied until the train came to a halt, the railroad bulls, of savage reputation, would surely find and arrest us or worse.

So I proceeded, Al following, to climb down the boxcar's steel ladder to the lower landing rung. When I thought I could keep up with the slow-moving train's momentum, I hopped off, running forward alongside the tracks to keep from falling. I came to a jolting halt along trackside when my hands slammed against a very big stone slab. It had been placed to mark the spot where Lincoln, on February 11, 1861, had delivered his good-bye to his fellow citizens as he departed to assume the presidency: "As I hope in your prayers you will commend me, I bid you an affectionate farewell."

This next is the last Civil War story. I found this 1864 gem in a collection of letters from a Michigan soldier to his family, this one to his father:

"Tomorrow is Christmas, and everybody at home is anticipating a happy time. I did not think I was such a home bird as I am.

"There is one thing, Father, I have been going to speak to you about from time to time, but have put it off. I will do so no longer. I want to ask your forgiveness for the many times I have been saucy to you. I see now that whatever the circumstances a Son ought never to sauce a parent. Whatever I may have said, Father, has been said to you in the heat of passion."

(*Sauce*, v.—to speak impertinently or saucily to. Informal.)

I haven't mentioned Thomas Jefferson and I must. Once I was trying to get a mental fix on that most enigmatic of our Founding Fathers, George Washington, when I ran across Jefferson's description of him. How about these excerpts:

His mind was great and powerful, without being of the very first order; his penetration strong, though not so acute as that of a Newton, Bacon, or Locke; and as far as he saw, no judgment was ever sounder. It was slow in operation, being little aided by invention or imagination, but sure in conclusion. . . . Perhaps the strongest feature in his character was prudence, never acting until every circumstance, every consideration, was maturely weighed; refraining if he saw a doubt, but, when once decided, going through with his purpose, whatever obstacles opposed. His integrity was most pure, his justice the most inflexible I have ever known, no motives of interest or consanguinity, of friendship or hatred, being able to bias his decision. . . .

His person, you know, was fine, his stature exactly what one would wish, his deportment easy, erect and noble; the best horseman of his age, and the most graceful figure that could be seen on horseback.

And I can believe this, too:

"His temper was naturally irritable and high toned; but reflection and resolution had obtained a firm and habitual ascendency over it. If ever, however, it broke its bonds, he was most tremendous in his wrath."

Old age provides time to read, or reread, such marvelous descriptive writing. And in Jefferson's case, we never tire of visiting his masterpiece, Monticello, probably the most fascinating home in all of America. A few years ago when we were in Charlottesville for a University of Virginia Miller Center meeting, we were invited by Kenneth Thompson, the director, to drive up the nearby mountaintop to Monticello for a lecture and buffet supper.

The lecture is long gone from memory. But sitting on Monticello's front porch, looking through Jefferson's automatic double glass doors, I saw the wind begin to blow beyond the house through whose far drawing-room windows we could just see in the late-afternoon light. Then I realized that in that drawing room there was a small table with two chairs, and on the table sat two of Jefferson's wineglasses and a decanter.

The droning of the speaker, the evening shower, some flying leaves, the chairs, decanter, and glasses created the illusion of seeing Jefferson and a friend engaged in earnest conversation as they sipped their wine. It was one of those mystic chords of memory that chance can provide for each of us, if we let our minds loose and our memories bubble to the surface of today.

Jefferson, too, worried about old age. "My only fear," he wrote when he was 58, "is that I may live too long. This would be a subject of dread to me."

In fact, he lived to 83, dying at Monticello on, yes, the Fourth of July on, again yes, the fiftieth anniversary of the signing of the Declaration of Independence, which was so largely his work and words. And in far away Quincy, Massachusetts, a fellow signer, John Adams, his old antagonist with whom he had made up, died that very same day at 90. Adams's self-consoling last words: "Thomas Jefferson survives." But Jefferson had died three hours earlier.

Lincoln was right: "we cannot escape history." It is every man's umbilical cord.

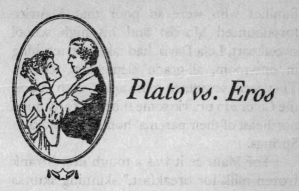

Plato vs. Eros

FIRE USUALLY BURNS UP family letters, photographs, family Bibles, marriage certificates, newspaper obituaries, all the detritus of life. This fire was different. It left behind, in the debris of my wife's niece's apartment, a big old-fashioned bread box. Inside, safe and unscorched, were all the Hall family ancestral photographs and a tiny notebook in which my wife's father, Maurice Crowther Hall, had kept a diary for the school year 1900–1901.

My wife had long been puzzled by two missing years between her parents' graduation from high school and their going to college. The diary disclosed that both had families who were so poor that Maurice (pronounced Morris) and his high school sweetheart, Lola Davis, had taken up teaching in one-room, all-grade elementary schools. They were seventeen miles apart, both out on the Colorado prairie some thirty or forty miles northeast of their parents' homes in Colorado Springs.

For Maurice it was a tough life: "drank frozen milk for breakfast," skinning skunks and coyotes for the pelts, catching a runaway team of horses, struggling with lazy and indifferent kids as well as bright ones, bicycling and plenty of hiking, too. But there were compensations: the Socialist Club, the Literary Society, the Debating Society, and lots of politics. "Bryan meeting in my school tonight." Colorado went for William Jennings Bryan over William McKinley; indeed, it favored Bryan in all three of his failed presidential campaigns.

But best of all for this young man of 19, as he recorded in his diary that turned up in the bread box, was his girl, Lola. Christmas holidays, 1900, meant meeting again back in Colorado Springs, skating in the evening at the Broadmoor, taking in school plays and an opera that cost $1.50 for two tickets. And there were long outings with relatives and friends and outings alone together. His diary, sparse as to emotions, finally gave us a glimpse of love on the prairies. "Went shooting in the afternoon. Started a discussion at night." Next day: "Went walking with Lola in the morning. Renewed discussion. Plato v. Eros. Arrived at partial settlement." It would be six years later, however, after college, that they married. Eros had to suffer Plato quite a while.

Love may be "a many splendored thing," but more often it's a war between the sexes. James Thurber had a lot of fun kidding about that war, but with strong undertones of truth. It seems to take a considerable yin-yang relationship to make a marriage last. So let's explore *Homo sapiens*, so called, a bit.

An anthropologist has said that human beings are faithful first to their species, next to their gender, then to their race. Think about it and it seems correct.

Reproduction of our species is our primordial urge, and it must have been working instinctively within me when I responded to Matthew's cry, way back in Chapter 1. Without thinking about it that way, I was simply helping to continue the human race, our species.

It's obvious, too, that over the millennia man has, more or less, conquered the other species on planet earth. Some species have been killed off ("dead as a dodo") others only held at bay. It seems to depend on what man, at any given time, perceives as the seriousness of the threat to his species. Currently, man must feel rather secure on this front because an Australian has invented the word *speciesism* to describe the attitude of those who sanction the slaughter of animals for human food and the use of animals for medical experimentation. Animal-protection groups argue that it is "wrong to inflict needless suffering on another being, even if that being were not a member of our species."

As to those species only held at bay, there is a never-ending war between man and creatures who attack the things man grows to eat and to clothe himself. And anyone who lives on the edge of the woods knows that the creeping vines will take over your house in due course if you don't look out, even though they may only be innocently seeking the sunshine. Consider how the jungle conquered Mayan temples in our hemisphere, Angkor Wat in another. Man may currently play king of the mountain, *Homo sapiens* triumphant, but it's a perilous perch as kings have come to know.

As to gender, it's obvious that the more

polygamously minded males have domi-
nated and controlled the more monoga-
mously minded females of our species. This
is not simply because of the biblical story of
Adam and Eve in the book of Genesis or
because of the male's muscular superiority.
It's because the female provides the means
of reproducing the species by a physical act
of the male's choice. And so the bulls among
us nurture and protect their females to as-
sure continuation of the species.

It is true that, historically speaking, in
the last few seconds of recorded history,
some females have managed to escape the
sheer biological jungle of this arrangement
and attain a stature as persons equal to the
male's, rather than serving simply as reproductive functioneers. But this is definitely
not the history of woman on earth, nor is it
true for most of the world's women today.

Publications are full of ads not just for
face-lifts, but also for skin peels, wrinkle
creams, breast implants for women (for men
there's something called ErecAid). The *de
minimis* swimsuits make the *Sports Illustrated*
annual issue a huge seller. And the latest
term in the public prints is "trophy wives" for
the young and beautiful successors to older
women cast aside by moneyed middle-aged

males. It's not quite like a hunter mounting a deer head on the wall, but it's not all that different, either.

Call all this sexist, sexual harassment or what you will. Feminists, militant and otherwise, have been fighting for some time now, but their success may be measured more in laws than in changed male attitudes. Still, things do change; there are even househusbands nowadays. But the biological differences between the genders that render males physically dominant remain the fact of life for the vast majority of our species.

I've often pondered why it's the male cardinal or peacock who has all the color and plumage to attract the female, a characteristic of the animal kingdom, yet among humans it's the females who wear the lipstick, perfume, and string bikinis.

Nora Ephron, a firsthand expert on the differences between men and women, questioned, "Can men and women be friends, or does sex always get in the way?" She did so in the hit movie *When Harry Meets Sally,* for which she wrote the screenplay. In an introduction to a paperback about the movie, she wrote that the truth is that "men don't want to be friends with women. . . . They want women as lovers, as wives, as mothers, but they're not really interested in them as friends. They have friends. Men are their friends."

Women, on the other hand, "are dying to be friends with men. Women know they don't understand men, and it bothers them: they think that if only they could be friends with them, they would understand them, and what's more (and this is their gravest mistake), it would help. Women think that if they could just understand men, they could *do something*. Women are always trying to do something. There are entire industries based on this premise, the most obvious one being the women's magazines."

I'd have to conclude, then, that the anthropologist is right that human beings are faithful to their gender, with the caveat that they are faithful in different fashions but nonetheless faithful because of their respective reproductive roles. If this is correct, probably the most we can hope for is more civility between genders. Their fundamental impulses are not going to change.

Finally, to complete the anthropologist's trio of species, gender, and race, consider race. Early on, male and female with their young, their elders, and other dependents formed the extended family that for so long has been the core of human society. Over time, families with something in common—tribe, language, color, religion, social status, particular skills, or combinations of one or more of these—gathered around powerful leaders. Feudal fiefdoms, city-states, and finally today's nation-states all evolved. Some of the earlier forms of association are constantly being replicated today, in racially homogenous urban gangs or simply in cohesive neighborhoods, for example. This is especially so in the massive agglomerations of modern urban life all over today's world, not just in America.

It has been *Homo sapiens* in the form of nation-states (a legacy from Napoleon, historians tell us) who has warred so often and so bloodily in this century now closing. We know that wartime hides, at least subdues, many of the normal divisions among men; gender and race are subsumed to survival of the species. Now that we have lived through the Cold War, we see that lifting of the Soviet-American bipolar control of so much of the world's interactions allows many of the old divisions among men to break out anew; a sort of new Balkanization of parts of Eastern Europe with the breakup of Yugoslavia as a vivid example.

HOW DID I GET HERE SO FAST?

In the last book she wrote, historian Barbara Tuchman included some pertinent observations. Discussing "two thousand years of human aggression," she concluded that, despite some "melioration" in human relationships, "the mold of the species is permanent. That is earth's burden." Amen.

Still, Tuchman did grant "melioration," however slow its pace. *Meliorate:* to grow better; improve. The American Constitution, especially its Bill of Rights, aims at melioration. All the legislative efforts to halt men's exploitation of man, male aggression toward females, to equalize the status of the races, to counter greed with compassion, flow from that effort by our Founding Fathers (all males, all white, many slave-owning, mostly well-to-do or rich).

"Melioration" applies to species, gender, race. Some believe in the perfectibility of man. I'd settle for the melioration of the way he behaves toward other species, the other gender, other races. Love and compassion are vital to melioration. Amen twice.

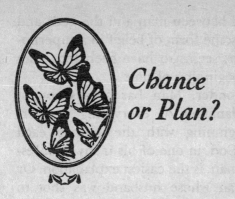

Chance
or Plan?

A FEW YEARS BACK, JUST prior to the upheavals in the communist world, I read a story from the Soviet Union describing a crowded Orthodox church service as composed of "mostly old women but some young people, too." I myself first saw those same "old women" in Russian churches in 1955—and again in 1965, 1975, and 1985. They never seemed to get any older. And there always were "some young people, too," who likewise seemed frozen in time.

As we would soon find out, all that anecdotal evidence for the death of religion in the Soviet Union was not very accurate. Religion, derived from the Latin and mean-

125

ing a bond between man and the gods and reflecting some form of belief in a superhuman power, seems to have been with man from the beginning of time.

No wonder. Man has always sought some explanation of everything he perceives, beginning with the sunrise each morning. God, in one of his many manifestations to man, is the easiest explanation. Or as a woman whose husband was shot to death put it: "I don't know why it happened. I can't say. At a time like this I have to keep my faith in God. Maybe it is destiny. God makes no mistakes."

Destiny, kismet, fate, chance, luck—or some superhuman plan? Some among us reach old age in no doubt whatsoever of the superhuman's plan. Others are still questing until the day they die. Some become so intrigued with the very idea they devote their lives to creating a philosophy or studying someone else's thoughts.

You can get very wrapped up in all this and end up arguing over how many angels can stand on the head of a pin. Historian Tuchman wrote of such "religious disputes, whose intramural fights are always the most passionate and venomous of any." Today we only have to look at almost any part of the globe to see adherents of Christianity, Islam, or Judaism taking to arms in the name of their religion or of some subdivision thereof. I have never seen any compilation of the total deaths in religious wars, only for some fragment of such conflicts.

My concern, now that I'm in my eighties, is with the world about us and how to explain its manifold mysteries. You don't have to lie on your back under a moonless night peering up at the galaxy of light in the sky overhead to wonder how it all came about and where it's all going. The photos of planet earth taken by our astronauts standing on the barren moon brought home the seemingly incredible fact that, as far as we now know, our earth alone sustains what we call human life. In a way, I think, those photos became the driving power behind our environmental movement. For the first time we had a sense of the fragility of our tiny planet within the vast celestial realm.

I confess an inability to comprehend it all, to find a rational explanation, to accept some superhuman power as having worked out the incredible number of animate things among us, not to mention mineral or vegetable; in short, the marvel of life on this planet alone.

"The world is not only queerer than we imagine—it is queerer than we can imagine," wrote J.B.S. Haldane, the British biologist and geneticist. I'll buy that. Or how about Albert Einstein? He spoke of a "rapturous amazement at the harmony of natural law, which reveals an intelligence of such superiority that, compared with it, all the systematic thinking and acting of human beings is an utterly insignificant reflection."

It is this kind of thinking that makes it so difficult for some of us to accept the idea that it all began with a "big bang." It is, somehow, easier to accept the idea that someday the sun will finally burn itself out and our planet will grow cold, and those living here then, millions of years after we're gone, will all die. It is even simpler and easier to think that man is so often so irrational that, having split the atom, he will set off enough nuclear weapons in some idiotic war between nation-states that the nuclear fallout will in a relatively short time wipe out all of us. Cicero noted that "no beast is more savage than man when possessed with power answerable to his rages."

Wendell Holmes at 93 received as a gift a book on the immortality of the soul. When Holmes's clerk, James Rowe, suggested reading it to him by asking, "Aren't you interested in the immortality of the soul?" Holmes replied, "No. I used to be when I was young, but now the subject bores me. Let's read that detective story."

Karl Marx, that intellectual father of communism, called religion "the opiate of the people," and his follower Vladimir I. Lenin, set out to make over the Soviet Union into a nation of atheists. Hence we used to be amused when some Kremlin leader was caught saying "only God knows."

Chou En-lai (or Zhou Enlai, by the new spelling), the longtime number two to Mao in China, once told journalist Harrison Salisbury that he thought chance was the main thing in man's affairs. "Paying lip service," as Salisbury put it, to Marx's theory of the inevitability of economic-social change, Chou said: "All events have an inevitable course, but it may be through an accidental turn that the inevitable happens."

Dean Rusk, eight years as secretary of state under Presidents Kennedy and Johnson, wrote in his autobiography that he had long been impressed with the role that "accident, chance, happenstance, the roll of the dice" had played in his life. We all can tell stories from our own experiences to illustrate this. I'll tell one myself.

Back in 1950, on a lovely Indian-summer day, I was strolling through Lafayette Park, opposite the front of the White House, en route to cover a hearing at the Federal Power Commission. As I ambled toward Andy Jackson on his ever-rearing steed, sirens began to wail. That's a usual city sound. However, these sirens were insistent, demanding my attention, especially when police cars came roaring round the nearest corner seemingly on two wheels. All were headed for the northwest corner of the White House.

The White House itself was being reconstructed, and President Truman was living across Pennsylvania Avenue in Blair House, the official residence for the nation's top-ranking guests. When I breathlessly reached Blair House, bodies and blood were everywhere. Two Puerto Rican nationalists had tried to storm Blair House to kill Truman, who was upstairs taking a postlunch nap. The blazing exchange of gunfire awakened the president, who incautiously peered through a window for an instant until guards shouted for him to get back out of range. The gunmen killed a White House policeman and wounded two other guards. In turn, one of the would-be assassins died on the bottom step leading to the front door, and the other fell wounded alongside a nearby hedge.

I was the first reporter on the scene. By chance, too, the *Washington Post*'s White House regular was taking a day off. And by another chance, all the other White House regular reporters were behind the Oval Office, out of sight, sitting in limousines waiting to go with Truman to an Arlington Cemetery ceremony. When my journalistic rival from the *Washington Star* finally ran up shouting at me "What happened?" I told him, or at least I like to think I did, "Tell you tomorrow, Jack." So chance put me on the main page-one story that night and gave me a big boost up the journalistic ladder.

And since we were talking a moment ago about Karl Marx, there is this Marx story. Maybe it was funnier before the collapse of communism, but I still cherish it.

It seems that a scholar, at the turn of the last century, was preparing a book on Marx, who had died in 1883. The scholar went to the British Museum to catch the atmosphere of the place where Marx had worked all those years researching and writing *The Communist Manifesto* (1847) and *Das Kapital* (1867 to his death). The scholar asked the chief librarian if, by any chance, there might be anyone still around the place who actually remembered seeing Marx in the library.

There was. The old man tottered in to be asked: "Do you happen to remember a man with a big beard who worked at this place, at this table, for many years a long time ago?" The old man scratched the stubble on his chin, then replied, "Why, yes, I do. I used to bring him a pile of books from the stacks every few days, and he would be buried in them until he asked for a new batch. It went on a very long, long time, and then one day he was gone. I often wondered whatever happened to that fellow."

Marx tried to construct, from the chaos of events, some sort of rationale, some general theory that explained it all. He came up with the inevitable triumph of "scientific socialism," of what he and we call communism; in short, economic determinism. In a way he was trying to do for man's interaction with man what a physical scientist does for the cosmos—and what religious leaders also do—find the laws that control everything. Arnold Toynbee tried to do the same in his *A Study of History* for the rise and fall of civilizations, but he had to distort too many facts to make them fit his straitjacket, historically speaking.

It seems evident to me that socio-economic laws are not very firm, that economics has not been called the dismal science for nothing, that chance plays a major role in all our lives and human destinies. Yes, some religions believe life is preordained, pre-destined, by some superhuman power. But not I.

It's similar for science. Certainly, if anything is certain, the most fascinating part of the human body is the brain. The way ours functions seems to set us apart from all other living creatures. We know something about the brain and we're constantly learning more. But there is still so much mystery about it. A young lady biochemist and I were discussing her work, and she mentioned the word *intuition*. I asked if she thought science would ever be able to unravel it. She thought not. And intuition is not alone among the mysteries.

Not long ago, as the communist world collapsed, Francis Fukuyama, a bright young man, wrote that "what we may be witnessing . . . is the end of history as such." This set off a furor. Narrowly defined as "mankind's ideological evolution and the evolution of Western liberal democracy as the final form of human government," history may be, just may be, no more, said to be at an "end." However, experience tells me, intuitively, that the evolution of the brain's thinking on this subject will continue and continue. That we've come to the "end" even in this narrow sense seems fantastic. We haven't even seen the end of human slavery. Just as our ancestors thought up new methods to carry on man's inhumanity to man, why should we think that even our contemporaries, let alone our successors, have reached any final thought on that subject?

One of the truly fascinating men of science in our time is Freeman Dyson, professor of physics at Princeton's Institute for Advanced Study. He published *Infinite in All Directions*, from which the following is drawn. The line that first hit me is the one about fingers and writing, but I want to quote four paragraphs to give a sense of his thoughts:

> To me, the most astounding fact in the universe, even more astounding than the flight of the Monarch butterfly, is the power of mind which drives my fingers as I write. Somehow, by natural processes still to-

tally mysterious, a million butterfly brains working together in a human skull have the power to dream, to calculate, to see and to hear, to speak and to listen, to translate thoughts and feelings into marks on paper which other brains can interpret. Mind, through the long course of evolution, has established itself as a moving force in our little corner of the universe.

It appears to me that the tendency of mind to infiltrate and control matter is a law of nature. This infiltration will not be permanently halted by any catastrophe or by any barrier that I can imagine. If our species does not choose to lead the way, others will do so, or may have already done so. If our species is extinguished, others will be wiser or luckier.

Mind is patient. Mind has waited for 3 billion years on this planet before composing its first string quartet. It may have to wait for another 3 billion years before it spreads all over the galaxy. I do not expect that it will have to wait so long. But if necessary, it will wait. The universe is like a fertile soil spread out all around us, ready for the seeds of mind to sprout and grow. Ultimately, late or soon, mind will come into its heritage.

My thinking is less stretched out than Professor Dyson's. I'm more impatient with the here and now.

I see a world full of tragedy as well as love. Holy wars, trumpeted as battles between good and evil, seem mostly to have been about power and domination, whether race, tribe, turf, nation-state, or alliances of nation-states. We've lived through forty-five years of Cold War alliance struggle. Think about the people who never made it through the Hundred Years' War. Or the Crusades, all nine of them, including the Children's Crusade. There was even a War of Jenkins's Ear.

Or look around us in America. Our democracy has been, is being, compromised by thieves, crooks, wheeler-dealers, unrestrained greed, cynical citizens and diminishing percentages of voters, elections manipulated by both big money and by engulfing television, as it used to be by powerful newspapers. You name the other problems. And yet nobody is hammering at the remaining gates of communism to get in; they all seem to think it's America whose opportunities are worth peril and trauma for them and their children.

Love, and acts of love, surround us. People do care. About our aging, about our children, about our homeless, about our country, about our environment, about our democracy. There is bonding between parent and child, and between child and grandparent, between Matthew and me.

There are, at least there have been, cycles in our national life of progressive movement forward, alternating with regressive steps, which seem to last the longer. Are we coming out of our long "me first" era into one marked more by compassion than greed? Are we once again going to be our brothers' keepers?

I do not believe in the perfectibility of man. But I do believe, in Lincoln's phrase, in "the better angels of our nature."

Democracy is imperfect by its very nature. Utopia lies always over the hill. Many religions promise an afterlife; they know that most of us will have a hard time on earth. But not for me. Maybe you'll remember that I'm hankering to be around for the year 2000, in my ninetieth year, to welcome the new millennium. How much more we'll know then than we know now!

Man, I'm going to miss this old world. It's so damned exciting, so full of fascination, so full of life.

Sources

HOW DO YOU FEEL ABOUT footnotes? Do you like them at the foot of the page they refer to or in the back of the book? And if at the back, should they be arranged by chapters or simply by pages? I think that, with rare exceptions, those on the same page interrupt the flow of the story, that they're better in the back. Then the reader can take them or leave them. I'm a taker.

In reading most nonfiction I use two place marks as I go along, usually reading the back matter as I begin or have just ended each chapter. So, if there's more detail in what follows than you care for, at least you have the explanation if you want it. I've tried to write these "sources" to include "where to find it," and frequently, something else that expands the text. Each begins with the textual page number to which it refers.

Preface. I cannot recall who first told me the Holmes-Brandeis story although I knew several of Holmes's latter-year law clerks. The story is retold on p. 31 of John S. Monagan's *The Grand Panjandrum: Mellow Years of Justice Holmes*, University Press of America, Lanham, MD, 1988, hereafter cited as Monagan. After reading my manuscript, Monagan has kindly given me permission to use the quotations from his book.

xii. The Holmes at 70 quote appears on p. 378 of *Yankee from Olympus* by Catherine Drinker Bowen, Little Brown and Company, Boston, 1944.

xii. The Whitman quote is from p. 24 of *A New Dictionary of Quotations*, selected and edited by H. L. Mencken, Alfred A. Knopf, New York, 1942, hereafter cited as Mencken.

5. The baby boomers data came from Fred Hollman of the U.S. Department of Commerce's Census Bureau, population division.

6. At least that's what Quayle's office told me on the phone, 1990.

7. The medical encyclopedia is *The Columbia University College of Physicians and Surgeons Complete Home Medical Guide,* Crown Publishers, New York, 1985. The quotes used are on pp. 263–65 under the heading "Common Complaints of Aging."

9. The Colorado governor was Richard Lamm (who didn't run for reelection). In 1984 he said that the old have "a duty to die and make way for the young." Quoted by Sandy Rovner in the *Washington Post* Health section, Oct. 17, 1989, p. 11.

9. Reference to British practice about kidney disease is from Spencer Rich in the *Washington Post,* Nov. 14, 1989, p. A-23 under the heading "Uncoiling the Medical Cost Spiral." The Swedish item comes from *Sweden Today,* an English-language government publication, but I foolishly cut it out without recording date or page.

9. The Court's "right to die" decision was handed down on June 25, 1990.

10. As to "greedy geezers," see *Newsweek* magazine's special Winter/Spring 1990 issue, "The 21st Century Family," article by Melinda Beck entitled "The Geezer Boom," p. 62.

10. Words to the poorhouse song, as quoted by Sandy Rovner in the *Washington Post* Health section, Aug. 21, 1990, p. 7, include:

> *For I'm old and I'm helpless and feeble*
> *The days of my youth have gone by*
> *Then over the hill to the poorhouse*
> *I wander alone there to die.*

From a George Catlin poem set to music in 1874.

12. The argument that social security is really a "welfare program" was perhaps best made by Robert J. Samuelson in *Newsweek*, April 18, 1988, p. 57. He subsequently reported a flood of angry mail from beneficiaries, but he has stuck to his guns.

12. The Krauthammer quote is from the *Washington Post*, June 19, 1988, opposite-editorial page.

14. "The Seven Ages of Man" appear in *As You Like It*, Act II, scene 7, as spoken by Jacques de Boys. I used the Yale Shakespeare text.

16. Average retirement age from *Modern Maturity*, June–July 1990, p. 32, quoting the General Accounting Office.

17. The Pentagon Papers story is well told in Sanford J. Ungar's *The Papers and the Papers,* E.P. Dutton & Co., New York, 1972. My role is in my *First Rough Draft: A Journalist's Journal of Our Times,* Praeger Publishers, New York, 1973, pp. 319–24, from which this account has largely been drawn.

21. Most of the papers I brought home ended up in the John F. Kennedy Library, Boston, where they are open to researchers.

22. Martin's autobiography is *It Seems Like Only Yesterday,* William Morrow and Company, New York, 1986. Quote on p. 65.

25. Emerson on happiness, Mencken, p. 511.

29. Cicero's *De Senectute* in English can easily be found in the *Harvard Classics,* vol. 9, 54th printing, 1961, p. 45. The excerpts I have used came from another translation I first used in a 1980 *Washington Post* article for which I lack a reference. The translation differs somewhat but not the points.

30. The Deng banner was reported from Beijing by Donald Southerland in the *Washington Post,* May 17, 1987, p. 12.

31. "King Solomon and King David" is in Mencken, p. 25.

33. The Copland quote from the *Washington Post,* Dec. 3, 1990, p. A10.

34. When Reagan entered the White House, I checked with the National Center for Health Statistics on his chances, in the mortality tables, of serving eight years. In 1980, a white male of 70 should have lived another eleven years. Since I'm three months older than Reagan, I was personally relieved to hear this.

36. AARP membership from its publication, *Modern Maturity,* for Dec. 1990/Jan. 1991, pp. 4 and 11 (where it is states that 27 percent of the membership is below the age of 60).

36. The Dominion Bank ad, offering "senior preferred banking," appeared several times during 1990 in the *Washington Post.*

38. Franklin's dialogue with the gout is reprinted from Carl Van Doren's excellent biography, *Benjamin Franklin,* Viking Press, New York 1938, pp. 633–34. I am indebted to Mark Schlefer for calling it to my attention.

40. The French red wine study from the *Washington Post* Health section, Dec. 4, 1990, p. 5.

42. Statistics about drivers' ages are from the June 1988 issue of *The Trailblazer,* published by the New Jersey Turnpike Authority, New Brunswick, NJ, and from *Time* magazine, Jan. 16, 1989, p. 28.

43. The "case-by-case" quote is from *Time*, above citation.

45. The doctor who told this story, Samuel Sanes, a Buffalo pathology professor, included it in his book *A Physician Faces Cancer Himself*, quoted by Victor Cohn in the *Washington Post* Health section, March 28, 1989, p. 11.

46. The feeling that one is fifteen years younger than reality is from "The Booming Business of Aging" by Ellen Berlow, the *Washington Post*, April 22, 1988, p. B5. Also used in *Newsweek*, April 23, 1990, p. 75. To illustrate the point the magazine reproduced an advertisement of a grandma showing her "Jockey for Her Pantyhose that Fit."

46. Life expectancy in the Iron and subsequent ages and current expectancy are from "Born to Age," an article on pp. 4–5 in the Spring-Summer 1981 issue of *Centerscope*, a publication of the Washington Hospital Center. This issue is devoted to "Understanding the Aging Process."

47. For life expectancy data see U.S. Bureau of the Census, Historical Statistics of the United States (constantly updated), and *Population Bulletin*, a publication of the private Population Reference Bureau. Census division of the elderly comes from the Census Bureau's population office, Washington. The gerontologists' division appeared in the *Washington Post*, Style Plus, May 11, 1989, p. C5. Here it is credited to Daniel Thursz, president of the National Council on the Aging, but Thursz told me that he did not originate it, that many gerontologists developed it.

48. The *Centerscope* article is in the Spring-Summer 1981 issue, p. 5.

52. From direct-mail advertising for *Longevity*, 1989, under the heading "the mind is . . . everything."

52. I can't find the Bliven article. But he did write an autobiography: *Five Million Words Later*, John Day, New York, 1971. He was a longtime editor of the *New Republic*.

53. Nor can I find the Astor biography by Maurce Collins. So just trust me on the bishop's dilemma.

57. I told the Henry Chalmers Roberts story in my *First Rough Draft*, As to the name Chalmers, I inherited it from my grandfather, Chalmers Thomas Roberts. *His* father, David H., did a peculiar thing: he reversed names to call one son Newton Isaac Roberts and named Grandpa after a famous Scottish divine, the Reverend Thomas Chalmers. But he didn't do the same for other sons Howard and Dwight. Howard, his wife, and son all perished in the great Johnstown flood of 1889.

58. I heard the Peck-Mason story on a TV tribute to Mason, but I neglected to record the date or program. Sorry.

58. Ann Landers's column in the *Washington Post,* May 20, 1988, p. G-4.

59. The jet pilot quote comes from Thomas Crook, and the National Institute of Aging specialist is Carol Fuchs. Both are quoted in the *AARP Bulletin,* April 1990, p. 2.

59-60. The Fairlie quote is from "Talkin' About My Generation," the *New Republic,* March 28, 1988, p. 20.

The tribute to Fairlie is by Andrew Sullivan, the *New Republic,* June 25, 1990, p. 43.

61. The Corcoran quote appears on p. 38 of *Portraits of American Presidents,* Volume I, edited by Kenneth W. Thompson, White Burkett Miller Center of Public Affairs, University of Virginia, University Press of America, 1982.

62. The Browning quotes are from his "Rabbi Ben Ezra" (1864), Mencken, p. 24. The Landor quote follows Browning's.

62. The Hepburn quote appeared in Chuck Conconi's "Personalities" column, the *Washington Post,* April 20, 1990, p. C-3.

63. The Moss Hart quote is on p. 421 of his *Act One: An Autobiography,* Random House, New York, 1959.

63. The Holmes-Pollock dinner story was recounted by Alger Hiss, then Holmes's law clerk, and appears in Monagan, p. 25. Holmes's remarks about being 80 are from Bowen's *Yankee from Olympus,* p. 393.

65. Ogden Nash's rhyme was quoted in the *Washington Post* Health section, Oct. 17, 1989, p. 11.

67. The sleep quote was by Dr. William Dement, in the *AARP Bulletin* for July-August 1989, p. 4.

67. The Churchill quote, as I give it, is an expansion of what he said on the same date, Nov. 2, 1949, as given in Kay Halle's *Irrepressible Churchill: A Treasury of Winston Churchill's Wit,* World Publishing Co., Cleveland and New York, 1966, p. 274: "Writing a book was an adventure. To begin with it was a toy, and amusement; then it became a mistress, and then a master, and then a tyrant."

67. The Zen quote comes from Carol Krucoff's article "Lapping It Up," in the

Washington Post Health section of June 5, 1990, p. 18.

70. Since using the "wealth of the Indies" quote, I've read it in John F. Kelly's article "The Writings on the Walls," in the *Washington Post* Weekend section, Nov. 9, 1990, p. 7. Kelly told me it came from James Boswell's life of Samuel Johnson, and in turn, that it was taken from a Spanish proverb.

71. La Rochefoucauld quote from his *Maxims*, Mencken, p. 23.

71. On sex among the elderly, see "Do You Know Where Your Grandparents Are?" by Sandy Rovner, the *Washington Post* Health section, Nov. 22, 1988, p. 12.

71. The Kinsey book was published by W.B. Saunders Co., Philadelphia and London, 1948. But the *Washington Post*, still locked in the old conventions, printed not a word about the book or its contents. The second report, on female sexuality, however, was announced on the *Post*'s page one when it was published in 1953.

71. The Princeton professor was John Gagnon, as quoted in a story from Stockholm about the Fourth International Conference on AIDS, appearing in the *Washington Post* Health section, June 21, 1988, p. 11.

72. The "miraculous" quote is by Robert Wright in the *New Republic*, July 11, 1988, p. 32.

72. The Donovan quote is on p. 37 of his *Right Places, Right Time*, Henry Holt and Company, New York, 1989.

74. Eating-out figures are from an undated but recent study by the Markle Foundation titled "Pioneers on the Frontier of Life: Aging in America." The pages aren't even numbered!

76. Moss Hart's quote, *Act One*, p. 212.

76. *Duologue* appeared in Jack Smith's column in the *Los Angeles Times*, Dec. 22, 1989, under the heading "Nice Duologue: Both Speak; No One Listens."

76. The Tannen quote is from her article in the *Washington Post* Outlook section of June 24, 1990, p. C-3. Tannen's best-selling book, *You Just Don't Understand: Women and Men in Conversation*, explores these sexual differences at great, if sometimes pedantic, length. Published by William Morrow and Company, New York, 1990.

77. Broder's quote is from his op-ed-page column in the *Washington Post*, July 3, 1988.

79. Two friends in their nineties are Dwight Salmon and Willard L. Thorp, who taught me history and economics at Amherst College, from which I graduated way back in 1933. They threaten to outlive my whole class.

80. "Old Ironsides" appears, among many places, in *We Hold These Truths* . . . , compiled by Francis Rufus Bellamy, Grosset & Dunlap, New York, 1942, p. 116.

80. The Holmes senior quote is in Mencken, p. 25.

82. Mrs. Holmes's bon mot is in Monagan, p. 52, and Bowen, p. 362. "Long and fervid relationship," Monagan, p. 71. "Available vices," Monagan, p. 26. "Low tastes," Monagan, p. 30. Holmes's letters were sold by her brother to the Harvard Law School Library after her death.

83. "Look them all over up and down" is from Monagan, p. 31. "I feel temperate," Monagan, p. 55. The law clerk was Richard Hale. On reaching 90 is on p. 342 in *Honorable Justice* by Sheldon M. Novick, Little Brown and Co., Boston, 1989.

84. The porch quote in Bowen is on p. 413. That from Novick on p. 283.

84. The Agnes Meyer story appears in her autobiographical *Out of These Roots*, Atlantic Monthly Press, Little Brown and Company, Boston, 1953, p. 172.

85. When I read on p. 34 of Katie Louchheim's *The Making of the New Deal* (Harvard University Press, 1983) Donald Hiss's account of driving Holmes to Fort Sumner, I wrote him to ask if they had visited Battery Alexander, the outer works of Sumner that directly overlooked the Potomac River. He replied that he could not recall that detail. It was of interest to me because Lois and I have been living for forty years in a house we built on the site of Battery Alexander. We have a photo from the Brady collection taken, probably in 1865, from where our terrace door is now located, looking upriver.

86. "Get down," Monagan, p. 42.

86. "Sonny, shake . . ." was told to me by Elizabeth Rowe, James Rowe's widow.

86. Holmes's ninetieth birthday is from Monagan, p. 139; Novick, p. 374; and Bowen, p. 408–10.

88. Hiss's account is on pp. 37–38 of Louchheim.

91. TR on Holmes is from Monagan, p. 52, and Bowen, p. 370. Holmes on TR, Bowen, p. 371.

92. Alice Roosevelt Longworth on FDR appears on p. 116 of my *The Washington Post: The First 100 Years*, Houghton Mifflin Co.,

Boston, 1977, and on the same page in the paperback edition titled *In the Shadow of Power: The Story of the Washington Post*, Seven Locks Press, Cabin John, MD/Washington, DC, 1989. As I recall it, Alice Longworth told the Dewey story over lunch during the 1952 Democratic national convention in Chicago.

93. The Evans obituary appears in the *Washington Post* of June 11, 1990.

93. Yardley's review appears in the *Washington Post Book World*, June 24, 1990, p. 3. The "vituperative behavior" quote is from the book Yardley was reviewing, *As Thousands Cheer: The Life of Irving Berlin*, by Laurence Bergeen, Viking, 1990. Incidentally, my daughter-in-law, Mary Higgins Roberts, has a grandmother who is 109. I had a spirited political conversation with her when she was 101.

94. The *Smithsonian* magazine article appeared in the January 1990 issue, p. 172.

94. The tombstone inscriptions are from *Grave Matters* collected by E. R. Stivstian (Ballantine, 1990) as reprinted in the *Washington Post*, Nov. 9, 1990, p. C-2.

95. The Fairlie quote (see page 59) is from the *New Republic*, March 28, 1988, p. 20.

97. The Kornhaber quote appeared in the *Washington Post* Style section of Sept. 9, 1988, p. B-5, taken from *Grandparents/Grandchildren: The Vital Connection* by Kornhaber with Kenneth L. Woodward, Transaction Publications, New Brunswick, NJ, 1984.

98. On Lincoln as a save-the-Union president see William Safire's novel of Lincoln and the Civil War, *Freedom*, Doubleday and Co., Garden City, NY, 1987. Safire's description of wartime Washington politics is especially illuminating.

98. My attention was first drawn to Lincoln's "mystic chords of memory" by a selection of his writings published in 1984 by the Book-of-the-Month Club, Inc., under the title *Abraham Lincoln, Mystic Chords of Memory*, edited by Larry Shapiro. This slender volume also contains the text of Lincoln's 1961 farewell address at Springfield.

102. *The Norman Rockwell Album*, Doubleday & Co., Garden City, NY, 1961. We first saw this drawing on the wall of a restaurant in a small Pennsylvania town and weren't happy until we found it in this book.

103. I must have thrown out the Moynihan quote, and his office wasn't able to come up with it, though they tried hard. Sorry again. But I have no doubts about its authenticity.

103. The non-Hispanic-white data on California appeared under Jay Matthews's byline in the *Washington Post* of Aug. 21, 1988, p. A-4.

103. The lady who complained in a letter published in the *Washington Post*, July 30, 1988, p. A-21, was Peggy Hull Caldwell.

104. Elizabeth Roderique Roberts (1768–1845) and her brother are buried in Lloyd's Cemetery, Ebensburg, PA.

106. On the Brady photographs of Lincoln, including the one engraved on the five-dollar bill, see *Lincoln, A Picture Story of His Life* by Stefan Lorant, Harper & Brothers, New York, 1957, and *Mr. Lincoln's Camera Man* by Roy Meredith, Charles Scribner's Sons, New York, 1946. Meredith says photo number 50, the five-dollar-bill original, was then owned by Mrs. Alice Cox. Brady's photo of the young Levin Handy is number 133 on p. 230. Unfortunately, Meredith's pages are often unnumbered, and he uses the same photo numbers for two sets of pictures. The Dolley Madison picture appears on p. 41 of *The White House* by Kenneth W. Leish, Newsweek Books, New York, 1972.

108. The Cambria County Historical Society in Ebensburg, PA, helped me greatly in trailing Grandpa Roberts. Grandpa Hall's story, as written down by his son, is now in my wife's possession. But alas, his diary, kept throughout the Civil War, is lost.

109. The Jubal Early story by Thomas A. Lewis appeared in *Smithsonian* magazine, July 1988, p. 66.

111. The "sauce" letter appeared in the *Washington Post* Outlook section, May 28, 1989, p. B-4.

112. Jefferson on Washington is from *The Life and Selected Writings of Thomas Jefferson,* edited by Adrienne Koch and William Peden, Modern Library, New York, 1944, p. 173–74.

114. Jefferson quote, Mencken, p. 24.

114. Adams quote, Mencken, p. 12, comes from the diary of his son, John Quincy Adams. The Lincoln quote is from his 1862 annual message to Congress.

115. Maurice Hall became a parasitologist, and it was he who discovered the cure for hookworm. That story is told in S. M. Lambert's *A Yankee Doctor in Paradise*, Little Brown and Co., Boston, 1946, pp. 100 and 142–43.

117. For the life of me, I can't find the clipping about that anthropologist. Sorry again.

118. *Speciesism* is a word created by Australian philosopher-ethicist Peter Singer, according to a column about him by Coleman

McCarthy on p. A-23 of the *Washington Post*, June 9, 1990. I do not, however, subscribe to the idea that man should halt use of animals in medical research.

120. The Ephron quotes are from the *Washington Post Book World* of Feb. 18, 1990, p. 15.

123. Tuchman quotes are from *The First Salute*, Alfred A. Knopf, New York, 1988, p. 300.

126. The quotes by the victim's wife are by Mary Clement in the *Washington Post*, July 6, 1988, p. B-1.

126. The Tuchman quote is on p. 36 of *The First Salute*.

128. The Haldane quote was attributed to Aldous Huxley in the *Washington Post* of May 22, 1988, whereupon reader S. O. Hashim in a letter to the editor said, no, "the words belong to the great British biologist and geneticist, J.B.S. Haldane (1892–1964)."

128. The Einstein quote appeared in an article by Eugene T. Mallove in the *Washington Post* Outlook section, Dec. 22, 1985, p. C-1.

128. Cicero quote: I can't find this one. Sorry yet again. But here's one I did find while searching: "Neither every wine nor every life turns to vinegar with age." It's from his *De Senectute*, quoted on p. 295 of

Dictionary of Quotations: Classical, Frederick Ungar Publishing Co., New York, undated.

128. Holmes on immortality of the soul, Monagan, p. 107.

129. The Chou En-lai quote is on p. 262 of Salisbury's *A Time of Change,* Harper & Row, New York, 1988.

129. The Rusk quote is from his *As I Saw It* as told to Richard Rusk, W.W. Norton & Company, New York, 1990, p. 611.

130. I've told the Truman story before in my *First Rough Draft,* pp. 94–95.

133. The young lady biochemist was Dorothy Beckett Fedarko, who had recently married a brother of one of my daughters-in-law.

133. Fukuyama's "end of history" essay appeared in the quarterly *National Interest,* summer 1989.

134. *Infinite in All Directions,* Harper & Row, New York, 1988. Excerpts appeared in the *Washington Post* Outlook section, April 3, 1988, p. B-3.

136. The War of Jenkins's Ear, 1739–41, a struggle between Britain and Spain, was declared by Britain after sea captain Robert Jenkins held up in the House of Commons an ear that he claimed had been sliced off by Spaniards, according to the *New Columbia Encyclopedia.*

Acknowledgments

FIRST OF ALL, THEY GO to my wife of fifty years (as of September 11, 1991). She has been my first editor on this and two previous books.

Second, to Ronald L. Goldfarb, a prominent, smart, and genial Washington attorney who, I think, has found it's even more fun to be an agent, and who sold my book to Warner.

Third, to my editor at Warner Books, Fredda Isaacson, who proved to be a gem. No picky-picky, just common-sense editing, transposing, inserting, adding, correcting. Curiously, it turned out that she, too, is a Pittsburgh native, though she attended

Schenley High School, the archrival of my own Peabody High. Maybe this mystic chord of memory brought us closer together in working on the manuscript. By the way, I wonder if the stairwell at Peabody still has the stained-glass window I mentioned on page 4. Somebody please tell me. And who wrote those lines?

Finally, to John S. Monagan for letting me quote from his book, as herein already acknowledged, and to Harvard University Press for allowing me to use the quotes from Katie Louchheim's *The Making of the New Deal.*